the lavender
envelope

the *lavender* envelope

approaching tomorrow by way of yesterday

jj hansen

WESTBOW
PRESS®
A DIVISION OF THOMAS NELSON
& ZONDERVAN

This book is a work of non-fiction. Unless otherwise noted, the author and the publisher make no explicit guarantees as to the accuracy of the information contained in this book and in some cases, names of people and places have been altered to protect their privacy.

WestBow Press books may be ordered through booksellers or by contacting:

WestBow Press
A Division of Thomas Nelson & Zondervan
1663 Liberty Drive
Bloomington, IN 47403
www.westbowpress.com
1 (866) 928-1240

Because of the dynamic nature of the Internet, any web addresses or links contained in this book may have changed since publication and may no longer be valid. The views expressed in this work are solely those of the author and do not necessarily reflect the views of the publisher, and the publisher hereby disclaims any responsibility for them.

Cover design: Angela McPherson
Cover art: Jade Alger

ISBN: 978-1-5127-8732-0 (sc)
ISBN: 978-1-5127-8733-7 (hc)
ISBN: 978-1-5127-8731-3 (e)

Library of Congress Control Number: 2017907849

Print information available on the last page.

WestBow Press rev. date: 07/31/2017

For those also on this journey of healing,
keep on; you are much less alone than you believe.

Contents

Preface

Dear Friend,

I wish I knew where on life's journey this moment finds you: be it a place of abounding joy so strong you feel as though rockets under your feet could propel you to the sun, a space of abandonment about ten feet from the earth's core, or somewhere in between. Regardless, my hope for you is that, as you read the essays between the covers of this book, you will find your thoughts turning to the collisions of your own life and your tender wounds scabbed over by time and distance, but far from healed.

For many years I thought what the Lord required of me was to act rationally, never be angry, and show the world I had gone on to live a successful life after the death of my parents. It took me six and a half years to gather the courage to turn that thinking on its head by writing these essays. Another year and a half passed in articulating and remembering. So here I go, after nine years, stepping forward to own the fact that I am still grieving, letting go, and working through the trauma of things I never wanted to see. Like Jonas, the Receiver of Memory who determines he cannot carry the memories of his people alone in the book *The Giver*, I have come to understand I was never meant to bear my memories and suffering by myself, to hold them inside for fear of causing others pain or betraying the ones I loved most.

My attempts to do this have only stifled my creativity and saddled my body with the most vicious form of chronic fatigue.

Hear me, though, when I say I still don't have the answers. I reckon with the fact that God is real, powerful, *and* compassionate. He promises to be the defender of orphans and widows in His holy habitation, and yet He is not the sort of defender who spares those in His charge from suffering so deep they would do almost anything to experience a few minutes' relief.

As I wrestle with profound paradoxes between truth and experience, I no longer have the patience for pat answers and explanations of why terrible things happen. In the deepest and darkest places of grief, those things didn't keep me. When I told God to get out of the driver's seat because He'd wrecked my life enough and I knew I couldn't do better, but I didn't really care, I wasn't drawn back from the precipice by the recitation of a few rote verses. It was the grace of God that, like an invisible tether attached between my shoulder blades, would not let me go, no matter how I swore at Him and sobbed. For that I will never have the words to articulate my gratitude.

If you're looking for a book with pretty words, pleasing images, and stories with happy endings, I don't have that to give you. What I have is the raw stories of my heart, an honest porthole into grief and the struggle to live, as I have known it. You see, I have come to learn this life is made up of many events we don't get to choose. Instead, we are faced with the decision to respond or react. Run, freeze, fight to survive, or face things head on, feel the pain, and live. The act of telling this story is, for me, a step in the direction of the latter. May your experience of reading it be the same.

Prologue

The Sealed Envelope

My first real published piece of writing was my mother's obituary. It was a strange writing assignment for an eighteen-year-old girl still in high school: sum up your mother's life in a few newspaper lines. Where do you begin a task like that? Sure, a three-second Google search reveals suggested formats, hints, and examples: Full name: Janet Gay Hansen. Age: 48. City: St. Paul, Minnesota. Date of death: March 27, 2008. Survived by: Husband Eric Hansen; daughters Lindsey and Jessie Hansen; parents; sister; brothers; nieces; nephews; almost everyone else. Visitation information, service information, interment, etc.—but how does this even begin to describe who she was? Add a few lines about her volunteer work with inner city children and women with crisis pregnancies. She was so much more than this, though.

Think, brain. Press through the fog and write something her brilliant life deserves. You're the writer in the family. No one else can articulate her life the way you can.

In the end I wrote something. My lawyer father added a few things, and the newspaper published exactly what I wrote because that's what my father paid them to do.

My uncle offered to put together a slideshow of pictures that would play during the visitation. He asked whether we wanted a black background or the dreadfully bright computer-generated shade of medium blue. Dad fiercely wanted this to be a celebration of her life and therefore vetoed the black. I tried to explain the black wouldn't show up and that it would blend in with the sides of the screen, making the pictures the focal point instead of the horrid blue. He held his ground, and Uncle Eric told me to let it go because it wasn't a big deal. It was a big deal, though, because Dad was being ridiculous and this service was supposed to be wonderful and classy—like my mom and the clothes I picked out for her, not like the loud animal or floral prints my dad sent into the dressing room whenever we went clothes shopping with Mom. How could her mahogany-colored wood coffin with her long wedding veil draped over it sit under a screen with photos framed by that awful blue?

I was so thankful Dad had decided to buy adjoining grave plots a few weeks before. All we had to do was meet with the funeral home and let the cemetery know to prepare the plot for burial. Dad and I met with the funeral planner before Lindsey flew in, about twelve hours after Mom died. We picked out the basic items—a wood coffin, a simple insert, a few overpriced floral arrangements—and gave the funeral home a comfortable velour sweat suit to bury her in. The ceremony wasn't going to have an open casket. We wanted people to remember her the way she lived in the photos and videos, not how she was at the end.

Friends offered to house extended family, so we figured out who was coming into town and matched each person with a place to stay. We chose the service date. We figured out how long to host the visitation before the service, picked our outfits, fielded phone calls, opened cards, and set up a floral display on the dining room table.

Little did I know, I would be grateful for this funeral planning experience five years later. I never dreamed it would be Lindsey and I shuddering under the weight of Dad's death, hardly sleeping, caffeinating ourselves just to keep our eyes open. How helpful it was to use the same funeral home, burial plot, headstone, and church, as well as base Dad's service off of an old program we'd kept from Mom's service. However, it was still too much. We were 23 and 27. The stress and responsibility was more than we could handle, but we didn't have a choice, so we squared our shoulders to the mirror each morning, painted on our faces, and kept going. Why? Because we loved our Dad. Because we were raised to be good daughters, to accept our responsibilities and do what is required of us even when we're ten seconds away from crumbling.

We planned a service, reserved the church, found musicians, orchestrated interment, wrote an obituary, and lined up people to speak at the service. We did these things because we didn't want to offend anyone, and we didn't have the voice to say, "No." Even if we had said no, who else would have done these things? He was our dad. It was our job. Plus, we didn't want to raise conflict and make things harder than they already were. So we kept silent. We zipped our lips, answered the next phone call, and sent the next email. We survived.

Survival became the theme of the next year and a half. It had been spoken over me in that first newspaper obituary and confirmed by the second: survived by: daughter Jessie J. Hansen. I felt it was my fate in life to endure a string of tragedies and hardships that would continue until my own heart stopped beating and *my* chest quit moving up and down. While others thrived, propelled forward by career successes and growing families, my family shriveled. I felt like I failed at my job almost every day, and I walked on with my gaze fixed to my feet—except for the moments I looked up at the sky, expecting to catch a glimpse of the next sole ready to smush me.

Ever since that day Mom entered the hospital to begin her treatment, I had been sucking it up and doing what I had to do. I pushed down the unacceptable emotions and played the part of the good daughter who trusted God in all things. I was the strong rock everyone praised for her faithfulness. The problem was, the things I stored down deep started to fester and multiply. They rose up; I pushed them down. They were too deadly to expose, too dirty to air out. If I let even one escape into the light of day, they would all come tumbling out of their carefully sealed envelope and make a mess of this life—no, call it existence—I was trying to hold together. True life belonged to those who didn't hold envelopes stuffed with the terror and horror of a scared sixteen-year-old, turned angry twenty-two-year-old, turned bitter twenty-five-year-old.

The thing is, I want to live.

I was created to write the stories of the living, not the dead. I'm tired of existing, dragging myself out of bed each morning because there is a to-do list to be done. I want to stop microwaving canned soup for meals and start throwing the vegetables I've chopped into a sizzling skillet. My body is yelling at me to quit thinking about what I should be doing and go climb a mountain, sucking in fresh air with each liberating step.

I long to cast the contents of this sealed envelope into the wind, to free my insides of all that has been held captive for so long. As I break its seal, I yearn to become an expression of the gloriously messy beauty that is the life I behold.

Section One

The Lavender Envelope

One day a little square envelope addressed to me arrived in the mailbox. I knew instantly it came from my mother, though the block-like print bore no resemblance to her cursive handwriting (a result of her post-chemo weakness, I suppose). The arrival of a letter was peculiar considering Mom lived a half-hour away in a hospital downtown and I had just seen her a few days ago. Inside the lavender envelope was a simple note. I still have it tucked away in my collection of finished journals. I wish I could remember all the words, but the part that shocked me was where she wrote something like this: "I don't really know how you're handling all of this."

I thought, *Yes, of course you don't know. And you never will, if I can help it.* It wasn't that I was angry with her or wanted control of the situation—not even that I didn't trust her. It was because she was suffering.

While I faced chemistry tests and history essays, she faced day after day of chemo and radiation treatments. When I began counting down the days until Christmas break, she started counting the first one hundred days after the adult stem-cell transplant. While I felt alive every time I inhaled the fresh, cold air of a Minnesota February, she wore a mask every time she left the house, for fear of the smallest piece of fungus invading her lungs.

It was *her* soft, thick brown hair that fell out strand by strand, clump by clump, while my long blonde locks remained fully intact. She was forced to have the last matted chunk of her hair cut off at the wig shop just weeks before she gave me money to get my hair cut. In time, her empty scalp grew dark, coarse chemo hair, and her smooth defined cheekbones gave rise to puffy, hairy cheeks. Meanwhile, I looked in the mirror and complained about the four pimples on my face. Her muscles disappeared, replaced by the weight of extra fluid built up in her tummy, while I lifted weights and ate massive plates of spaghetti to improve my moves on the basketball court.

How could I tell her I steeled my innards on I-94 every time Dad and I drove to visit her? Or that I didn't like hugging her anymore because her once warm and embracing hugs had become frail and bony? What could ever possess me to confess I said "I love you, too" every time she said it, but I no longer felt it?

No, I couldn't reveal these things. As long as they remained hidden inside, I could pretend on the outside that I was still the daughter I used to be.

The thing was, we had both changed, my mother and I. The woman who greeted me at each hospital visit wasn't my mother. This woman's name was Janet Gay Hansen. She was married to Eric Peter Hansen. Her parents' names were Martin and Shirley. She had two daughters. She sometimes sounded like my mom. But this was not my mother. My mother was a nurturer. When I came home from school every day, I would lie on the couch with my head in her lap and tell her about my day. As I talked, she would use her long, motherly fingernails to pick the earwax out of my ears. (A doctor once said to me upon examination of my ears, "My, aren't you a waxy girl?" This was four years after my mother had died. I can only imagine the buildup.)

When I was home sick from school, my mother would

make me ring noodles with butter and run to the store to pick up Powerade for me. When I had my wisdom teeth surgically removed during my freshman year of high school, Mom signed up to chaperone my volunteering group so that she could dispense my prescription pain meds on schedule, thereby allowing me to participate. She attended every volleyball game I ever played, every band and choir concert, every musical I was in, every basketball game—until her address changed and she started sleeping alone in a hospital bed in a sealed room. She would have come to every tennis match I played if she could have. I know she wanted to be there.

Mom delighted in being with us because quality time was her most meaningful love language. On game nights, we played my dad's old version of Clue (the pictures of the characters looked like cartoon drawings), the Game of Life, Skunk, Phase 10, or Rummikub. Sometimes we watched movies, or my dad would set up the slide projector and screen to show us a bunch of slides from a recent family trip. (He didn't convert from slide film until 2008, refusing on the principle that the resolution of slides was so much better than prints. In 2008, he soared into modern technology with the purchase of a digital camera, completely skipping prints altogether.) However, my mother almost never made it through an entire movie or slideshow without having to get up to switch a load of laundry, start the dishwasher, or attend to some other household task. She always said, "Don't worry about waiting for me," but Dad always stopped and waited for Mom. We'd sit silently in the dark, the room illuminated by the glowing TV monitor or slide projector screen, until Mom returned.

Mom loved people. At heart, I think she was still more introverted than extroverted, preferring smaller gatherings of people or one-on-one lunch dates, but she loved being with people. Where my dad was task-oriented—making a list of things to do each day on a three-by-five card and transferring undone things from one day to the next—my mom was people-oriented. Uncle Eric still tells stories about how every time he visited, dinner was late. Dad would get so frustrated, but the pattern never changed. Mom would start chopping vegetables at the island while talking to her brother. However, her rhythm would look something like this: Chop. Listen ... listen ... listen ... chop. Chop ... listen ... listen ... listen, and so on and so forth.

Mom was a pretty good cook, though. One of my favorite things she made was homemade chicken noodle soup. She used a whole chicken carcass and simmered it on the stove for hours. I also loved her chicken and wild rice casserole. Growing up in the freezing North where winter lasts almost half the year, we ate a lot of hearty casseroles—not to mention that wild rice only costs half an arm and a toe to buy up there.

My mom had the best laugh. Lindsey and I especially loved to make her laugh so hard she'd cry. (We not-so-creatively dubbed it the "cry laugh.") It all started one night when Lindsey and I were teenagers. We began dancing around the kitchen and singing in two-part harmony, "Daisy, Daisy, give me your answer, do. / I'm half crazy all for the love of you. / It won't be a stylish marriage, I can't afford a carriage. / But you'll look sweet upon the seat of a bicycle built for two!" We had Mom laughing so hard it looked like she was weeping, and tears were streaming down her face.

A few years ago, Lindsey was visiting me in Chattanooga. We were hanging out with my Chattanooga "family," and my Mexican "dad," *Papi*, got Lindsey laughing so hard her face screwed up like she was really upset. All of a sudden, I said, "You're doing the cry laugh!" It was a pretty great moment as Lindsey wiped the tears from her face and tried to compose herself enough to appreciate the reality that the cry laugh had not died with Mom but lived on in her. We later learned I inherited it as well. We're quite a pair when we really get going—and it doesn't take much to get us going.

This was my mother: the woman whose name literally means, "God's gracious gift showing a lively mood." I was named after her, the uninhibited woman who danced around the kitchen island singing Messianic Jewish music with us. This woman was never too serious to "boing" bellies with me for a good laugh (even though we didn't like the Teletubbies). She knew her way around a sewing machine well enough to make me a dog costume like my friend Kayla's (although she accidentally bought black-and-white cow-print fabric instead of Dalmatian print). When I asked for a pioneer-themed birthday party, she made it happen with gunny-sack races, water pail–carrying relays, and a cake with a Conestoga wagon hand-drawn on it. The safest, warmest place in the world was inside one of her hugs. She even loved me enough to tell me when I needed to start shaving my armpits and that it was okay to take two showers a day in the height of my high school basketball career.

How could I embrace the woman before me who was a shadow of the one I loved? How could I reach for her when I was staggering back from the blow of her suffering?

12-5-06; Day 7 of 100

My Dearest Jessie,

When you called me the other day and said, "Hello, Mama," it made me feel like you were going to curl up in a chair and lean against my side. I was sorry you came home early from school since you felt bad.

Anyway things have gone well since the stem-cell transplant, and I have been feeling very good to this point. How do you feel about me being sick? I really can't tell how you feel about it.

I'm happy about how your basketball season is starting out.

I have loved every stage of your growing up. I love being your Mama.

Love, OOOXXX
Mom

Quitting Number 20

It was November 2007 when I walked into Coach's office, my best friend Alli at my side, armed with my teenaged version of liquid courage (white chocolate raspberry mocha from Caribou Coffee). In seconds the official words were going to come out of my mouth: "I'm not coming to basketball practice this afternoon, or tomorrow, or ever again. I'm quitting basketball."

The night before, I had cried on the phone with Alli as I told her that I felt like God was leading me to quit basketball. My mom's health was so unpredictable. It had been almost a year since the transplant, but her body still hadn't accepted the adult stem cells, so she was living a very isolated life at home to protect her compromised immune system. Every time the doctors tried to wean her off the immune suppressant drugs, she reached a certain level and the stem cells attacked again.

Something in me said I didn't know what was going to happen with her, so I couldn't justify spending two extra hours a day away from home. I didn't talk to my parents about it ahead of time. I had been pretty much taking care of myself for the last year, so I felt like it was up to me to make the call. My dad confirmed that when I got home after school and delivered my news right there in front of the hostas. He quit trimming for a minute, looked at me, and asked if I really wanted to do this. When I said, "Yes," he said, "Okay, well it's your decision."

I never questioned my choice to quit after that day, though there were days I cried over it. It wasn't so much missing the sweaty passing drills, "suicides" (a form of conditioning torture as well as disciplinary action), shooting practice, and box-out drills. It was the team. After I told Coach I was quitting, he told me if I changed my mind at any point, jersey number 20 would be waiting for me. He understood. He had grown up with a handicapped father who died sooner than he should have, so he knew the weight of impending loss and grief. More than once in the coming months I landed in his office, pouring out the struggle of surviving, and he challenged me to quit numbing and embrace the pain. He said I had to face it; I said I couldn't. He said I'd have to deal with it at some point; I said (to myself), *Yeah, but not today.*

Coach asked me to go to practice after school and tell the team myself, so I did. I entered the big, fluorescent-lit gym and cut across the wood floor toward the stage, where everyone gathered to tie shoes and stretch before practice. They were dressed in long basketball shorts, T-shirts with the arms cut off, and headbands made from pre-wrap; I wore khaki pants and a monogramed polo. Once everybody was there I looked into the eyes of these girls I had spent ten hours a week sweating, kidding, and laughing with and yelling "Ball! Ball!! I'm open!" at four months out of the year. I told them I was bowing out. I wasn't going to any more practices or games. My basketball career was done. They responded with the kind of group hug only a slew of female basketball players could accomplish, their strength and tenderness squashing my brave façade.

The team didn't quit supporting me just because I quit playing. They were there the day Dad picked me up from school and told me Mom's lungs were 80 percent covered in fungus. As he talked to one of our coaches, I told him I needed to go do something, and I took off toward the gym. I ran into practice and through gaps in tears told them the latest update. They heard what I wasn't saying.

I didn't make it to most of their games, but I was there for the game they won to get to the state tournament. I rode to the arena with the students from school but hopped down to sit on the bench and take stats. I wanted to be with them, to encourage from the front lines and share in the victory of my team. I was at their first game in the state tournament when they played at the Excel Energy Center, too. I was there, but I couldn't be with them. The security staff patrolling the edges of the floor wouldn't let me near the team because I didn't have a badge. I went to the bathroom and cried, and then I went back out to the student section and acted like it didn't matter.

The girls on the team were there for me until they weren't. Not necessarily by choice, but they couldn't be because, while our paths had crossed for so long, mine split off when I quit basketball and theirs kept going in that direction. Their lives continued on, and I felt like mine stopped when I got off the basketball train. I quit because I felt like I didn't know what would happen with my mom and didn't want to be gone from home so much; I never imagined I would start to feel trapped and suffocated in my own home.

While Mom was in the hospital, I froze my emotions in the car on the way there so that I wouldn't break down or cry or feel anything while I was with her. When I got home I would step into the shower and cry it all out, or just feel the familiar empty painful ache where no tears would come. But once Mom came home, there was no car ride to "freeze" my insides on the way to visit her, and the periods of being around her and trying not to feel anything were so much longer because she was now almost always home. I couldn't handle being so close to her frail body and struggling immune system, so I found other places to be. I went over to Sarah's house for hours in the evening, working on Spanish homework, but mostly talking and hanging out. In the spring, I signed up to be a manager for the boys' baseball team with my friends. That was the straw that broke the camel's back. (I didn't consult Mom and Dad before making that decision and going to the first game either.) Mom and Dad sat me down in the living room, and Dad said it was almost like I didn't want to be at home with them. Mom cried. I had no words that would express to them how trapped I felt in my own house without breaking Mom's heart and eliciting Dad's anger.

I don't know why I didn't consider joining the basketball team again once I started to feel stuck at home. Maybe it was because another girl on the team began wearing jersey number 20. I might have felt life itself was too much to handle, even without that extra commitment. It could have been because I had made my decision that cold November morning when I walked into Coach's office, and there was no going back. But I think the real reason is that in my eighteen-year-old mind, the only way I knew how to love my mom was by quitting basketball.

Mom, Did You Hear Me?

Mom,

    I went to a wedding last Saturday, and it made me think of you. I remembered how we used to watch "A Wedding Story" on TLC every afternoon in the summers—how you cried at so many of the episodes. I wondered, though, what really made you cry? Was it the special moments in the strangers' lives being portrayed on the TV screen before us, or was it the glimpse you had of these precious days and moments that would come in your daughters' lives? Were you looking forward to the future and crying with happiness, yet sadness, at the day your daughters would pledge to become one with a man and exchange his last name for yours and Dad's? When you knew that you weren't going to beat the graft-versus-host disease, did you cry because you would miss that day and all the happy and sad days in between and all the joyous and rotten days to follow?

    I cried. I cried the week of my seventeenth birthday when you were in the hospital undergoing chemo and radiation, struggling through the initial stages of the year-and-a-half battle you would fight. It was my birthday, and birthdays are a big deal, but there was no extra excitement or special preparation to celebrate my birth, because as the anniversary approached, the family focus was on preventing your death. And so I wailed. I wailed so hard I couldn't stand, my knees pressing into the bedroom carpet as I rocked forward and backward in a vain reach for comfort.

I snotted and sobbed under the branches of a large oak in a cemetery next to Big Springs Baptist Church in South Dakota. I tried to keep it together through choir practice that afternoon, because we were on tour and I needed to be okay, but when Mrs. Holmquist stopped everyone from singing and started talking about how we needed to sing "Precious Lord, Take My Hand" from the deep places of our hearts, I couldn't stop the tears from coming. When she started talking about what it meant to her—how she had to pray every morning for the Lord to take her hand and lead her on—I had to start wiping and sniffing in a futile attempt to stem the tide. When she looked at me and said, "Jessie knows what this is like," I lost it. I ran out of the church and into the cemetery. I folded myself into the deep depression on the side of that oak as I let all the tears and snot flow. Over heaving sighs and gasps for air, I could hear Alli yelling my name as she tried to find me. I had told her more than anyone else, but I didn't want to be found, even by her.

I bawled the night I came home from senior trip when everyone else's parents were waiting to meet them as the bus pulled into the parking lot. I don't remember if the tears welled up on my drive home, while I was making dinner for one, or if they waited until I arrived at the cemetery. What I do remember is my tears when I found your grave and you weren't there. A polished, engraved piece of stone rested in the ground in front of me, marking a place where a hole had been dug and a cement vault had been built to keep the ground from settling when the box that held your body started to decompose.

Mom, did you hear me in the last days, those final hours, when you were in the coma? They say hearing is the last sense to go. Could you hear the things I said when I came to visit the hospital alone at night? Did you hear me tell you that I really did love you? Was my voice interrupted by the soft tears dripping from my chin? Could you feel my cold hand in your warm one, even though it was so puffy with fluid? Did you know I was there just hours before your heart stopped? I hope you know I wanted to stay longer. I just couldn't do it. I didn't know that was the last time. Did you? I wonder if you felt your heart stop, if their attempts to wrestle you back into this life were painful, or if Jesus met you and whisked you away from the suffering within the walls of that room. By the time we got there, you were gone. I lifted the hand your lifeblood used to flow through and my kiss met cold skin. Could you see us in those moments?

Do you know how much we already missed you in the fog of our shock? I couldn't go back to sleep when we got home. I came downstairs to watch TV just in time to hear Dad call your parents from the other room. Did you hear how he broke down when he said the words, "Janet's gone"? All his love for you poured out in the sobs that wracked his body as he stood in the dark dining room.

Mom, losing you and the process of losing you destroyed me. It was like a bomb exploding in slow motion, more and more pieces of shrapnel ripping through me each time I saw you suffering and in pain; each time you weren't there for something important; each time I sat at play practice, opening and shutting the curtain and crying alone in the dark because Dad was on a date and my heart hurt and no one else was supposed to know.

When I went off to Drake, I was scared of leaving the only place I'd ever known as home and the people I loved, yet so ready to be in a place where I could be treated like a normal college kid—not have everyone know (or think they knew) all about what had happened to you. I remember feeling like I had to protect people from finding out that you were gone because I knew they'd feel bad.

When Dad was coming down for my birthday at the end of September, a floor mate asked why you weren't coming. I told her you couldn't be there. She kept going on about my mom not coming for my birthday. I did everything I could to not have to speak the words "She's not coming because she's dead." After I rushed a sorority, though, and ended up not joining because I couldn't afford it, I was talking to a guy on my floor that I had a crush on. I said something about how my roommate's mom felt about us rushing, and he asked me what my mom said. I told him flat out, "I don't have a mom." I think I was tired of not saying it. I still couldn't bring myself to declare you were dead, though. When I did say something, I used phrases like "passed away" or "I lost you" or whatever other combination of words came to mind, but I couldn't utter the word *dead*. It seemed so final and real. I couldn't say it until I went to Spain. There was something about expressing it in another language that made it easier. "*Mi madre ha muerto*" didn't quite carry the finality and reality of "My mom is dead."

I often tell people that things would have looked different if you had still been here when I graduated from college. I think I would have moved back to Minnesota instead of moving to Chattanooga, or you and Dad would have moved south to be near Lindsey or me.

I wonder if you would have bugged us to join a singles group at church because you and Dad found each other that way, or been on the lookout for nice young men to introduce to us. Honestly, though, part of me thinks we would have already gotten married by now, maybe even started our own families, if it weren't for losing you and Dad. Grief and trauma have been the heaviest of wet blankets, drowning out the vivaciousness and free-flowing laughter of our true selves.

Sometimes I picture sitting across the table from you in the mid-morning sun, with our coffee cups in hand, breathing in grace and peace, exhaling words about life. I imagine calling you on my way home from work to tell you about a particularly impressive accomplishment, or perhaps just my exciting weekend plans. I do have to wonder, though, how these last several years would have been different if you were still here. I wonder if I would have had the courage to take two years off from working full time, start a business, and write a collection of essays about grief. I never would have chosen these things on my own.

I think I've told everyone but you how much I hate the fact that my kids will never know Grandma Janet (or maybe if we all lived in the South, it would've been whatever form of "Nana Janet" my children could pronounce), except in pictures, the distorted voices of home videos, and the stories I tell them. It grieves me to think they will never feel your tender arms and soft hands cradle them close and know your deep love for them. They may never know what they're missing, but I know. I know how amazing your hugs were, how fun it was to make you laugh so hard you'd weep. I also know how much you wanted to embrace the man I vow to love through all the days of this crazy adventure we call life.

Mom, I don't know how to lose you. I didn't know at eighteen, and I'm still trying to figure it out at twenty-seven. I learned to function without you, but I don't know how to lose you—how to love you and your memories with all that I am and embrace everything you've taught me, while letting you go. How do I release the pain and suffering that came from the way your life ended so I can begin to live again?

Section Two

Eye of the Hurricane

Shortly after my mother's death, I told myself the hurricane was over, sunny skies must be ahead. Surely Dad would walk Lindsey and I down the aisle at our weddings, become Grandpa Eric in a matter of years, and then adventure around the country with our families. Life could never be the same without Mom, but somehow we would pick up the debris around us and build a family again. Of course all of this was subconscious. I didn't write it in my journal or speak it aloud. I didn't even realize I believed it until the eye of the hurricane moved on.

People who have weathered hurricanes before know about the eye: the deceivingly calm place in the middle of the storm where the winds are whipping so fast and hard around it that everything is still. Even a fifth grader doing a project on hurricanes for the school science fair can identify it. However, someone who has never experienced a hurricane or researched it would have every reason to believe the storm was over when he entered the eye.

This being my first encounter with such a storm sweeping into my nuclear family, I naturally let down my guard somewhere inside the eye. A true novice, I began to unlatch the shutters and take away the sandbags. I threw open the windows to let fresh air into the house and danced outside in the bright sunshine. I told others about the hurricane I had weathered and rejoiced that I survived with my home mostly intact and an opportunity to rise again.

As a result, I was completely unprepared for the phone call I received in August of 2012. It was the year I was supposed to have graduated from college, started my first "real" job, and furnished my own apartment like a true young adult. Instead, because of my early college graduation, I had just celebrated my one-year anniversary of working for a discipleship program in Tennessee. I lived in a furnished apartment on campus and was about to celebrate my 23rd birthday. Over the previous year my job had been helping women identify the pain that had driven them to addiction, and in the process, I realized the depth of my own unhealed wounds. Together we had been healing, my students and I. When I looked at myself in the mirror, I felt beautiful, and I eagerly anticipated the months and years that lay ahead.

I was visiting a friend of mine in Knoxville, Tennessee, when I talked to my dad that day—the day I heard the old familiar howl of hurricane winds. I was sitting on her front porch in the warm summer morning air as I noticed something different in the tone of Dad's voice. He told me he hadn't been feeling well and that his abdomen had grown round despite his lack of appetite for several weeks. This was strange for him because my dad had been thin all his life, with a healthy appreciation for food, and religiously weighed himself to make sure he didn't gain weight. He explained a variety of things could be the cause; he didn't have to be specific. I knew a real possibility was cancer, so I braced myself again. The wailing wind I heard in the distance was louder than the echoes of my memories. I knew how this story played out. We had been here before, my dad and I. I knew firsthand what happens in hurricanes.

Following the cancer confirmation a few weeks later, the eye wall made impact. I was visiting Dad for Labor Day weekend, and he filled me in as we sat on the balcony of his condo, watching the sun set over the marsh. It was colon cancer—stage four. It was so aggressive it had grown from nothing to metastasizing throughout his body in a year. He told me all about the chemo, diet changes, and natural supplements he would begin, both of us thankful that this type of chemo would only produce neuropathy and nausea so his soft blond hair would remain intact. For the rest of the weekend Eagle Scout Eric talked positively, declaring the Lord had this in His hands, all the while preparing Lindsey and I for the storm ahead, with envelopes containing official documents, access to the safe deposit box at the bank, and making sure we knew how to sail our little sailboat back and forth across the lake at the cabin. The hurricane was back.

For the next month I woke up every morning, showed up to work when I needed to, called to check in on Dad, and attended church on Sundays. I was on autopilot, and I didn't even know it, not until a friend of mine challenged me to live in the midst of what was going on, not just check out and wait for it to be over.

The only problem was that in order to live, I had to deal with emotions—emotions I didn't want to experience. I was furious at this hurricane that had overtaken me. I had grown up loving and serving Jesus since I was five years old. I had clung to Him when my mom was sick. Many nights I wasn't able to fall asleep over the roar of the wind and waves of this internal storm, until I found a promise loud enough to drown them out for one more day. I repeated over and over to myself the words of King David and the declarations of Isaiah. *I almost fainted but I didn't, because I believe I will see the goodness of the Lord in my life. When I enter into the deep waters He will be right there guiding me through. When I cross rushing rivers, their currents will not be able to sweep me off my feet and carry me away.*

However, this time the rumble of the storm was so loud that the repetition of those verses was nothing more than the moving of lips. There was no sense or reason in my father's cancer diagnosis just four years after losing my mother. None of my friends from high school or college had weathered the death of a parent, and here I was poised to lose my dad and become an orphan at twenty-three. Why didn't they feel the effects of the wind and rain? How come they didn't dread the rising floodwaters?

It wasn't fair.

Life wasn't supposed to be this way. I didn't sign up for this. When I wrote in my journal as a high school student that I would follow God the rest of my life, come fire or high water, I didn't mean this.

I raged and cried and penned eight pages of handwritten lament, but I had no beautiful revelation. No scriptural prayer or exhortation suddenly came to mind and ministered to my heart. When I called a dear friend who had lost her father to cancer a year prior, she didn't answer the phone.

I was alone.

Even the miraculous provision I had seen from the Lord during my mother's sickness waned as reports on my father rose and fell. As a teenager, I had completed college-level papers, sports practices, laundry, and cooking on five or six hours of sleep, but now I was exhausted all the time, even though I wasn't taking care of my father—or even living with him for that matter.

I dragged myself out of bed in the mornings no matter how many hours I had slept. This was not new to me. I had dealt with it before, in spurts of a few months at a time, this unrelenting fatigue that fogged up my brain and left me emotionally unable to make decisions. This time it wasn't fading, though. My body was betraying me. Every emotion I refused to deal with, every bit of trauma I was carrying, my subconscious brain released as fatigue to "protect" me in my vulnerable time. I was stuck in "fight or flight" mode, except that I was actually in "freeze" (nature's third response) where fatigue, anxiety, and depression took turns having their way.

The backside of the storm had caught me unaware. I barely had time to run inside and scramble on top of the tallest piece of furniture that would hold me. In moments it was there: the dirty, swirling water seeping into my house in the absence of the sandbags that had blocked most of it before. The open shutters clattered against the siding as I shivered on top of the table, my eyes trained helplessly on the rising water, one moment hoping against hope it wouldn't reach me and the next moment determined that if it did, I would find a way to climb higher.

Dragonfly

The average adult dragonfly's life spans no more than a few short months. After spending up to five years underwater as a nymph in the aquatic larval stage, it crawls to the surface, sheds its skin, and begins to fly. In the coming days and weeks it will mate, and the female dragonfly will deposit her eggs somewhere in the water to hatch. She will die without ever seeing one of her offspring. Similarly, the male dragonfly's life will end with nothing more than a biological link to its descendants. The next generation will hatch and grow, with instinct alone as its guide.

How fortunate we are that as human beings our lifespans allow for generations to live side by side together, witnessing each other's lives and learning from the experiences of those who have gone before us. For me, instinct took over on the drives down I-94 to visit Mom in the hospital. It kicked into high gear, though, in the cancer ward of Abbot Northwestern hospital. For the first time in my life I was given the task to love with all the fervor I could muster one who had nothing to offer me aside from bony hugs, frail smiles, denial, and an occasional frustrated outburst. In this place the expression of love took on a whole new face. Recitation of poetry would have been less than appropriate. Fifty kisses a day couldn't fix things—forget gushing or flattery. The question was, could I remain physically present until the end?

I was there. When the call came, I dropped everything.

I knew what awaited me in Minnesota, but I didn't rush. I methodically purchased a plane ticket, repacked a suitcase I had only just unpacked from a nine-day jaunt to Turkey, and made sure to include a matching black skirt and blouse. As I sat on the plane in a fog, I couldn't help but hate the reason I was flying north.

When I arrived in the city, I was met with panic and steeled nerves. Panic came through the phone from my stepmom, because Dad's nurse unwittingly messed up his medications and was freaking out about his condition. The steeled nerves were all mine as my best friend from high school sped toward the hospital, determined I wouldn't be too late this time.

I wasn't quite prepared for the frail little man who met me inside that hospital room. Only six months before I had cooked a Christmas Eve feast for him and Lindsey. He was too thin then, but when he hugged me with his six-foot self, it was strong and safe. He smiled and laughed and called me "Jessie Jo." I even convinced him to read my favorite childhood book, *Ruby the Copycat*, one night before we went to bed so I could record the way he read it, pronouncing "R-u-b-y" as "Shooby-dooby-Rrrruby." I offered to spend my vacation time on another visit, but he insisted that I would just sit there while he didn't feel well. No, I should go visit my dear friend in Turkey, and then let him feast on the stories. Come May, that's exactly what I did. The day after I returned I regaled him with tale after tale of rich cultural experiences and native Turks we met. It wasn't until I finished and we had enjoyed every morsel of my travel stories that he told me his cancer markers were higher than I knew possible. And it was two days later, May 30, when the doctors told my stepmom there was no time to waste in calling his daughters.

Here I was. Lindsey was on her way from the airport, so I greeted him first, surprised when my kiss met scruff before landing on his cheek. His cheeks had always been so smooth, unless he'd forgotten to bring his razor to the cabin for a long weekend. The skin that used to stretch across his face in a smile now sagged, and his nose jutted out from underneath the bridge of his glasses. His hair looked more gray than the handsome blond it had always been, and his toes stuck up from under the covers. Red socks served as a visible reminder to the nurses that he was a fall risk.

This wasn't the strong man who showed me how to split firewood and drive a boat. He couldn't be the one in the photograph balancing on the bongo board with infant me in his arms. It must have been someone else that carried me in a hiking pack up the volcanoes in Hawaii, shot hoops in the driveway, and played tennis in the shadows of the Sedona red rocks. Oh, to be with him in one of those places again!

But here we were. And it was my dad. He was confused, though, because the cancer had crusted around his intestines, so his body couldn't process the gas building up inside. Instead, it had gone up to his brain, turning this sharp lawyer into a bewildered patient. He was so nauseated that he couldn't eat, but even if he could have kept from throwing up food, his frozen digestive track couldn't have processed it. Every bit of ice chip he spooned into his dry mouth was sucked out of his stomach by the G-tube so that he wouldn't throw up the water and bile.

Deep down I had known it would come to this. Where else could the path lead once the words "stage four cancer" were uttered? My gut feeling had been confirmed in March when Dad went home early from a vacation because he knew something was wrong. This time the doctors discovered his markers were ten or twenty times higher than they had been at the beginning. He told me all about the new chemo he was starting and how God was in control, and then he said, "You know I love you more than words can say." And I knew. That little sentence—the one that might sound like a precious expression of love to someone else—told me everything. My dad often told me he loved me, but he always said, "I love you." That was it. As much as he didn't want to believe it and fought the notion with everything inside him, I wonder if he knew even then where the road would lead. Did he know what was coming in a few short months?

The next morning when we arrived at the hospital, Dad was sitting up, reading the newspaper, and talking to the nurse about the trip he took to visit me when I was studying abroad in Spain. We couldn't believe the improvement. This was my dad. This was the man I ran to greet when he came home from work. He was the one who taught me how to paddle a canoe, build a retaining wall, and sauté shrimp. He called me "Shrimps" and "Sparkles" and "Jessie Jo" and greeted me with a hug at least once a day when we were in the same state.

There was just one problem: Dad appeared to be on the mend, but the cancer still had a vice grip on his intestines, and his liver was shutting down. Liver failure meant chemo was no longer an option, and immobile intestines meant he couldn't absorb nutrition or poop. (For months the word *stool* did not conjure up an image in my mind of a tall chair.)

But he felt fine. The drugs the doctors had given him so far had been successful in removing the gas from his brain and the pain from his body, so his analytical mind was at full tilt. The assurance from one of the doctors about his "leaving" the hospital in a few weeks didn't help either. Lindsey became so mad that the doctor wouldn't just speak plainly with him. She needed to tell him his body organs were shutting down, the cancer was winning, and there was nothing they could do. He was dying.

How do you tell a man who feels mostly fine that he's dying? How can you tell him he's run out of time for dancing and laughing and playing with his step-granddaughters? What do you say to convince a man who wants more than anything to live to sign a paper invoking a DNR so that he can go to a hospice facility and die in "peace"? How do you explain to his friends that they need to come see him because he doesn't have much time, when he just sent them an email saying he's in the hospital for a few days and he'll have to postpone Thursday's golf outing?

But there was one night. One night was different. Lindsey and I were sitting with him; one of us on each side of the mechanically adjusting bed. He looked at us and said he wished this was happening farther down the pike, but he knew we'd be okay. We were independent and smart, and we'd made lives for ourselves. He said the best job he ever had was being our dad and that he wanted me to have his skinny-necked Epiphone guitar. He even made us promise to make sure someone played cribbage with one of our stepbrothers at family functions, because he knew how much he liked to play cribbage.

We thought he was going that night, so I took my chance to share with him a few songs I'd written on the guitar. After I played and sang, he said they were really good, but it was his next words that I had waited years to hear. He told me the lower range of my voice had matured well, and I didn't have to push the notes out—that my voice was beautiful. I had always strived to be as good as my sister in his eyes. I wanted him to praise my voice like hers and buy the CDs for my school concerts, too. He never said I didn't have a good voice but never quite gave the praise I wanted, until that night.

A few days later, the morning of June 8, we arrived at the hospital bright and early for Dad's transport to a hospice home. My face flushed and I held back tears at the scene we encountered. Three nurses were crying as they tried to help Dad into his clothes. He was so weak and in so much pain that he was agitated, and no matter what they did, it hurt him. Once they helped him onto the stretcher and I found my way to the car, I let go, but by then the tears wouldn't come.

All morning Dad had been saying something that sounded like, "Hasha." He was having trouble speaking, the gas built up again on his brain. We thought we knew what he was saying but pretended we didn't understand. See, for several years Dad had been going to an alternative doctor. Throughout the cancer battle, Dad had continued to consult the alternative doctor as well as the traditional oncologist. This doctor encouraged my dad to take all sorts of supplements that might help fight the cancer, claiming they were safe to take with chemo. Some days Dad was taking sixty different capsules. What the alternative doctor didn't tell Dad was that his liver had to process every supplement he swallowed and every bit of chemo that drained through his port. So in the hospital, when the oncologist said there was nothing more they could do because my dad's liver was failing, Dad asked about taking a milkweed thistle supplement, because that is supposed to help the liver function. He didn't understand that his liver didn't have the power to break down the supplement that would supposedly help it.

What the alternative doctor did tell my dad months prior was that a particular treatment that had seen some success with another type of cancer could maybe help my dad and that if it didn't help, it certainly wouldn't hurt. What the assistant who administered the treatment did say to Dad was, "When modern medicine gives up on you, come to us. We can heal you." Her name was Sasha. One morning when my stepmom had gone on Dad's laptop in the hospital room to send an email for him, she noticed there was an unsent message from the middle of the night. It was a note addressed to Sasha, pleading for help. At one point Dad even proposed going home from the hospital, buying one of those machines that cost around twenty-thousand dollars, and hiring Sasha to give him the treatments at home.

We did not believe Sasha could heal my dad. And so without a word spoken between us, every time he breathed out "Hasha," we pretended we didn't understand what he was saying.

Walking down the silent wide hallways toward Dad's new hospice room, I noticed a colored glass dragonfly hung on each room number. Thoughts of dragonflies flew from my mind, though, when my distraught stepmom greeted me at the door, pouring out the story of what had happened while I stepped out to make a phone call. After I left, Dad suddenly yelled, "I gotta get out of here!" and swung his legs over the side of the bed, trying to get out. Her five-foot-two frame had barely caught him before he hit the floor and she screamed for help. The nurses came running, gave him a shot of something to settle him down, and put him back in bed. Thankfully, that was the last of his distraught outbursts.

He stayed quiet after that, his little body dressed in a light blue hospital gown. There was no need for glasses anymore. His eyes were closed, and his skin was so yellow, the jaundice claiming a stronger hold as his liver continued to fail. I couldn't help but note the irony that I came into this world with jaundice and here he was leaving with it.

Grandpa Martin, Mom's dad, arrived for a visit that afternoon. Grandpa had spent years volunteering at the hospital as a chaplain, so he knew all about how to be with dying people. He came right up to the bed, unafraid, and tenderly took Dad's hand in his. Leaning close to Dad's closed eyes, he said loudly and clearly, "Eric, it's your Dad, Martin, here from Terre Haute, Indiana. It's so good to see you, son. Can you squeeze my hand? There you go! I know you can hear me." Even though Mom had died five years earlier, Grandpa didn't love Dad any less. He was one of his sons, and he loved him as such. Grandpa then led us in worship, his unwavering voice rising and falling with the melodies of a few steadfast hymns.

An hour or so later Dad's breathing changed. We responded to the phone call quickly, and when we arrived, his breaths were slow, the space between them growing longer and longer. When we moved close to say our last few words, I told him I had one more song to sing. It had come to me as I was preparing to head north just over a week before. Leaning close, holding his hand, I sang.

> Farewell, I will love you still.
> Farewell, from the bottom of my heart.
> Farewell, I will love you still.
> No matter where you are, you're always in my heart.

Through our tears, we followed that song with several more hymns. Finally, he took that last breath. We weren't sure it was the last until the nurse slowly walked to the head of the bed and listened for a few seconds with her stethoscope. As the warmth of his life began to fade, I turned away from Dad's body and found one of my stepbrothers. Hugging him hard, I said Dad loved him like a son, but the truth was that he loved him *as* his son. Dad told the nurse in the hospital he had three boys, three girls, and two granddaughters. He had poured the life and love of a father into all his children and grandchildren, regardless of biological links.

After several minutes the nurse motioned for us to join her outside the room, drawing our attention to the glass dragonfly hanging on Dad's room number. How fitting that it was blue, his favorite color. My stepmom wanted to keep it, but the nurse gently led us to a huge wall in the atrium and said we had to return the dragonfly to where it came from. Several other bright yellow, dark pink, and emerald ones were scattered across the metal mesh. I wondered how many dragonflies had returned to the wall that day as we chose the best place to release ours. Finally, we let go of the smooth rounded body belonging to this larger-than-life blue dragonfly.

Letting Go

I began letting go of my mother as an eighteen-year-old girl in a hospital room at Fairview Medical Center. It was nine o'clock at night and I was alone, but I had come with Dad so many times that I knew exactly what to do. I drove the little maroon Saab 9000 west on I-94 through St. Paul and into Minneapolis, exiting at Heron Boulevard. I don't recall what occupied my thoughts as I rode the silent elevator up to the fourth floor of the hospital and turned into unit B, but I still remember pushing the large doors open and striding down the hallway, pausing to scrub my hands at the sink outside Mom's room. The lights were low as I entered, casting an eerie yet strangely peaceful glow across the room. The beep and sigh of the machines keeping Mom alive were a blessed change from the gargle of blood-filled lungs trying to breathe and the panic of unabated pain saturating the room. The nurse in the corner made little noise as he monitored my mother and her machines.

Coming around the side of the bed closest to the window, I pushed play for a CD of hymns we left there, the instrumental melodies filling the room. In this moment I allowed my tears to gently drip onto Mom's hand as I held it in mine, my thoughts turning to the future and all the events she would miss. The words came in spurts from my mouth, phrase by phrase, all starting with "I'm going to miss."

I couldn't stay long because of the smell. Everything else had become peaceful compared with the traumatic weeks preceding this one, but the smell in the room hadn't changed. It lingered—a smell far from body odor or gas. She hadn't had solid food since before the trach tube invaded her windpipe, before the ventilator started breathing for her, so there was no solid waste leaving her body. But that smell, that bitter unnamable scent had permeated the room, and I stayed until it almost infiltrated me. I had only been there about thirty or forty minutes and I wanted to stay longer, but I just couldn't. I had said my piece, stroked her hand, released my tears, and about six and a half hours later her heart beat for the last time as she let go.

I started letting go of my father the day he told me something was wrong. I knew what the coming months would bring, even if it was only because I expected the worst. During that last week in the hospital—just a few miles from the room where I visited my mother that final evening—I let go of hope that my father's healing would come on this earth. I let go and I encouraged him to let go, to sign the DNR and trust that God wouldn't be so cruel as to let him die in such a way the doctors could have revived him right after he changed his medical directive.

Dad was caught between two terrible medical realities: cancer crippling his body, which called for more chemotherapy, and a failing liver which prevented his body from being able to receive any benefit from the chemo. He was a fighter. We were fighters. If we could have engaged the cancer in hand-to-hand combat, we would have—but we couldn't. There was nothing more we could do, nothing more he could do. It was time to let go.

I hit a wall in the letting go a month and a half after Dad died. Lindsey and I were standing in my storage unit in Minnesota, and I was opening box after box of childhood things, trying to whittle down the "keep" pile to the number of things I could fit in the Dodge Grand Caravan I had rented to cart the rest of my belongings back to Tennessee. We had already spent several days going through Dad's storage unit on the other side of town, working as a team to sort, pack, and donate the contents. This side of town was different, though. The decision-making was solely up to me, and my powers of discernment were freezing up like an overtaxed machine. As I stood in this two hundred square foot storage mansion between a towering bookcase and a stack of tubs as tall as me, the wheels in my head spun. Staring into a box of childhood stuffed animals I had spent years hugging and playing with, I began to cry.

"I hate this," I said. Lindsey heard what I was really trying to say and gently told me to shut the box and take all of them.

That day in the storage unit was like the first family trip we took without Mom. Dad took us out to Oregon, and we spent a week walking Agate Beach, visiting waterfalls, eating seafood, and reconnecting with a few relatives. At the end of one long day of driving, we sat at the hotel, and Lindsey began to tell Dad how upset she was about how fast he had driven around the curvy roads that day. She got more and more upset as he defended himself and didn't validate her point of view. When she began to sob, I started crying and finally interpreted for Dad: "It's not about the driving. She misses Mom!"

It's been four years since that day in the storage unit, and I'm still letting go of things. It took me a year to relinquish Dad's five-sizes-too-big, sheepskin-lined slippers, even though I had my own pair of furry moccasins that fit just right. Two years passed before I donated the baby clothes Mom saved from when I was a child, even though I would never choose to put them on my own children. I still can't seem to let go of Dad's childhood chest of drawers that held my summer clothes when I lived in the house on Rae Lane. It's too small for me as an adult and one of the drawers is starting to come apart, but when I replaced it, I couldn't bear to give it away.

While we were cleaning out the garage at the cabin, I found myself keeping the dirty weed bucket I always found hideous, because I could so clearly picture Dad walking up the hill from the backyard, his work jeans splattered with paint and dirt, holding the spade in one hand and yellow weed bucket in the other. I can still see him handing me the bucket and telling me he'd give me a penny for every dandelion I picked and his look of complete surprise when I returned and asked for $10.

I have learned that people are not their things, and I know keeping Dad's weed bucket won't bring him back. However, attached to things are memories. If I give away the hideous weed bucket, what will remind me of working in the yard with Dad on Saturdays? How will I remember the lesson in thoroughness I learned weeding the row of prolific buckthorn bushes? Will I remember how first Mom and then I planted pink and purple petunias by the lamppost every spring?

I could never forget my parents, but what if I forget the stories of the life we spent together and the stories of their lives before me? What if my children never know the legacy of their grandfather's hard work or his lifelong love of learning? What if they never hear about the matching Christmas dresses their grandma made for Lindsey and me or the amazing holiday spreads she set out on the dining room table?

When I face the mirror and see blonde hair, it came from him. I look into my blue eyes, and he's there. Because of his Norwegian heritage, I've followed in his footsteps to the dermatologist every year for a mole check. Ask me for my full name, and you'll get his, too. Ask me what I know about golf, basketball, tennis, football, and skiing, and there's at least a 90 percent chance I learned it from him. I am my father's daughter.

Every time someone says my name, my mother's name is uttered: "Jessie," the Scottish pet name for "Janet." When I smile, there she is. When I laugh so hard it looks like I'm weeping, she did it first. When I extend grace to others in the midst of conflict and anger, it's because she told me time and again, "People are precious." Grandpa says our talks on the phone remind him of his Sunday afternoon phone calls with Mom. Uncle Eric says I have her nature. Kathy says she hears my mother's voice in how I talk about the way the Lord is leading me. I am my mother's daughter.

What if that isn't enough? Who will carry on the Hansen name when Lindsey and I sign marriage licenses? What if my boys have dark brown hair and olive-toned skin, and my daughters wear their father's smile? What if I never have any children at all?

If I let go of these things and pry my last finger from the ones I have loved so dearly, who will remember?

Section Three

Arrows

I'm not angry. I promise. I'm not. Sure, I've been angry a few times. I mean, I've spent most of the last nine years walking in, through, or out of the valley of the shadow of death. I watched my father honor his vow to have and to hold my mother in sickness and in health until death parted them. I watched my stepmother love and cherish my father until death parted them. In the wake of these events I have plowed furrows for grace, forgiveness, and love that cost more than I had to spare. Inch by inch I plowed, sweating profusely, choosing again and again to cast aside the seeds of bitterness and anger. I am above that. Anger can't trap me. I've moved on.

I've moved on. Look at me. I have more than a quarter of a century to my credit. A certificate for a bachelor of arts in English writing sits on my desk as proof of my academic achievements at a private university. I spent a semester learning the language and culture of Spaniards and traveling Europe. For three and a half years after graduation I worked in full-time ministry, helping men and women walk out of addiction and into freedom. Oh, and now I've checked Asia off my list of continents I've visited, in addition to North America, Europe, and Africa. I drive a cute and sporty, red Nissan Sentra named Charlee (which means "to be free"). I wear skinny pants and tall boots with cotton blazers or tunics and cardigans. I shop at Aldi and Publix, where I buy organic free-range whole chickens to cook in my crockpot and carrots, celery, and onions to make chicken stock from scratch with the carcasses. I live in a quaint old house lined with ancient crepe myrtles, in a historically significant city surrounded by beautiful mountains and rolling hills, in a country that is the land of the free and the home of the brave. So what could I possibly have to be angry about?

What is the point of feeling anger? What does it actually accomplish? Who can say they're better off for having been angry? Who wants to be angry? Why can't I release all the frenetic energy in my chest that's turning my face red in one arrow carefully drawn with experienced precision and released off a cliff into oblivion?

When I was a kid, I went to Pioneer Girls' camp several times. I always took archery as one of my activities. During class my instructor showed me how to slide the guard over my left arm to protect it, and I worked on lifting the bow to eye level, holding it steady as I gently drew the bowstring back. I practiced letting go smoothly and watching the arrow as it flew toward the target. Despite my efforts, each time I raised, drew, and released I had to go and retrieve an arrow from the outer edges of the target or pull one out of the ground in front of it. For every time I wore an arm guard and carefully positioned it just so, the bruise on my arm grew darker as the bowstring grazed past.

Some people shoot angry arrows at other people. Usually the longer they've been doing it, the more accurate their aim appears. However, they are rarely actually shooting at the right targets, preferring instead to shoot at the close ones only (the ones they're guaranteed to hit). Others, like me, mostly refuse to pick up the bow. Isn't that the surest way to make certain a human target is never hit? That way I can prevent things from getting more messed up and ensure no one else sees the barbaric nature hidden deep inside.

Every time I do pick up the bow and shoot off into an unoccupied part of the forest, my arrows are like boomerangs—they come back every time. So why continue to shoot them? Wouldn't it be better to just carry them safely on my back in a quiver where they won't hurt anyone? That takes less effort than firing them into the woods over and over again.

Okay, so yeah, I guess I'm a little angry. I'm angry that nine years after my mom died, I'm still struggling with the aftermath and unhealthy patterns triggered by her sickness and death. I resent the fact that my sister has attended a counseling session or two and had "good cries" as she drives here or there, while I have spent thousands of dollars and hundreds of hours in pursuit of physical and emotional healing, weeping for hours at a time, unable to remove the dagger of grief from my chest.

How could I feel anything less than betrayal when several friends from high school weren't available while my dad was in the hospital dying and I needed them? It was unconscionable for them to turn around and spend my precious time at the wake wanting to hear all the details, preventing me from having a chance to talk to my dad's old coworkers who took half a day off work to come and didn't have my phone number to reach me at another time. I'm still appalled that people had the nerve to approach me with guilty tears running down their faces because they hadn't followed up to see how Dad was doing and therefore weren't prepared for him to die. Why did I comfort them when my dad's body was laying in the casket in one of his nice suits that was too big because he couldn't keep the weight on when the chemo treatments made him sick? Fury doesn't even begin to describe what surfaced after the numbness wore off and I came face to face with the reality that just five years after I tossed a red rose onto my mother's wooden casket and watched them lower it into the ground, I stood on top of her grassed-over grave with Dad's gaping open in front of me.

I'm angry about things that haven't happened yet, too—things that will never be. It is every bit unjust that the man who wants to spend his life with me won't be able to ask for my parents' blessing to marry me. It's not fair that we won't have to outfit the first row of chairs at our weddings with a tissue box, like Lindsey and I always joked, because Mom won't be there to need it. I fight angry, bitter victim tears every time I watch a father/daughter dance, because my dad and I were supposed to cut up the floor with our swing dancing skills.

Who gave death the right to steal all this?

I was supposed to visit my parents and drink coffee with Mom in the mornings. She always said we would. When I have my first baby, Mom was supposed to come help me figure out which cry means what and how to soothe each one. Dad was supposed to take in all the little faces my little one will make and say, "That's it! You made that face when you were little." Even if they didn't live close by, they should at least be a phone call away at 2:00 a.m. when a little one won't stop crying and I've tried everything and I feel like I'm losing my mind—but they won't be there.

I'm angry about the places I've found myself in the last nine years, too. I never wanted to believe there could be a trench of pain and grief so deep that God himself would remain silent and nothing the griever could do would have the power to make Him speak. How could a faithful follower ever reach such a degree of desperation that she lives for hot shower water on her back because it's the only thing she can feel stronger than the searing pain trapped inside her chest? Surely it's unthinkable that one who has pledged her life in service to the One she loves could spend days wishing she didn't exist anymore.

How does one escape victimhood in this place?

What does one do with the knowledge that perfect love

drives out fear when she cries out night after night to be loved and feels nothing? How does she respond to the terror of yet another thing going wrong and one of the final places of her life that's gone all right coming apart at the seams?

Her quiver is so heavy. The strap cuts into her shoulder as she carries it up the mountain so steep she must forge her own trail of switchbacks. The trees are so thick that she can't see the valley below or mountaintop above. Most days the sunlight cannot clearly penetrate the foliage above her head. She knows she was created to fly, but even if she had wings, she could never lift off the ground with this crushing quiver, growing in weight day by day. She cannot continue. She must fire the arrows. Around her she hears the call and response of forest creatures. Silencing one of their songs with her arrows is unthinkable. If she must release an arrow, what is to be the target? Who could withstand such a piercing wound? Who would be willing to suffer with her, for her?

She has heard stories of one whose back was torn to shreds by a raging whip, whose hands and feet still bear the scars of firsthand encounter with death. Pondering what she's heard about this carpenter, she perches on a large rock next to a spring, sliding an arrow from the quiver. As she fingers its sharp point and smooth shaft, the memory floods back, and suddenly she's returned to the place where she picked it up. She hears the words that were spoken, feels the surge of emotion inside. This time, however, she suppresses the urge to stuff the arrow back into the quiver. As the rage grows from red to white inside her chest, the heat spreads to her face. She feels as though she could throw the boulder she sits on right down the mountainside. She lifts her bow to silence a crow that has shrieked one too many times, but when she draws the bowstring back, the arrow drops in her lap. It has shrunk to a fraction of its original size, and the arrowhead has become dull. Perplexed, she feels the roaring internal fire slowly subsiding to smoldering coals. Casting the arrow aside, she plunges her hands into the cool water, splashing it over her face and hair and then slurping it from dirty, cupped hands. Rising, she shoulders the heavy quiver and continues a few steps farther until it is time to release yet another arrow.

(If) I Could (I Would) Just Scream

I'm so angry I could just scream. But I can't. I can't scream, because my roommate just got out of the shower, and I have neighbors who live below me and next to me; if I screamed, they would come running to find out what was wrong.

If I could, I would, though. I would scream so hard and long for all the frustration of a healing process that takes way too long and doesn't guarantee completion. I would scream because of the anxiety ball that's taken residence in my chest ... again ... for the umpteenth time, after I've worked so hard to convince my body that it doesn't have to be in "alert" or "survival" mode.

I would scream because I'm so frustrated that I keep on failing, and I'm so afraid that one of these days I won't be able to fail any farther, because I've already fallen as far as I can go and there's no getting up. I would scream because I just want to be able to function like a normal human being, and yet I'm incapable of doing such a simple thing as paying my credit card bill on time or putting away clean clothes after I wash them or even feeding myself three healthy meals a day. I think I will scream if one more person suggests a little trick to having more energy, like taking vitamin C every day or drinking forty ounces of water each morning before eating.

I want to scream because I just can't take it anymore. I can't handle riding the seesaw between overwhelming anxiety and depression, lighting on the balance of peace and joy for mere seconds in between. Is four years not enough to figure out how to keep papers from collecting on the floor and desk and put clean clothes away after they've dried and find places for all the things that belonged to Dad or Mom or Mom's mom or Dad's dad, which I can't seem to let go of, yet they are clogging up my life and choking me from the inside out?

Isn't it enough time to sort through seven thousand slides and figure out which ones to keep and digitize and which to toss? Surely it's sufficient time to downsize from eight boxes of childhood toys and memorabilia to two. Yet, somehow it's not even long enough to find a bigger filing cabinet so that the stack of papers that doesn't have room to be filed won't surpass a foot and a half.

They say, "Slow and steady wins the race," but what about when slow turns to not steady and not steady turns to stuck? What about when a leg cramp sets in on mile two of the marathon and by mile eight collapse is imminent? And who wants to spend her whole life racing toward the finish line of a never-ending, always-growing to-do list?

If I could, I would scream.

That's the difference between Mom and me. She didn't process things quickly and often froze when several tasks presented at the same time, but she could scream. She didn't do it often, but every once in a while she'd get so upset about something that she'd say, "I'm so upset, I could just scream!" and then she'd follow it up with a high pitched, "Ahhhhhh!!!" Usually Lindsey and I responded by laughing (privately) because she was the only person I ever knew who really screamed after saying something like that. Now I wonder if it actually helped her release the stress and tension. I could use some of that relief myself. If only I could scream.

(If) I Could (I Would) Just Scream

For a long time, when I would get really, really, scared or severely startled, I would go absolutely mute. I'm not a big fan of rollercoasters, and the few times I have been dragged onto large ones, not a single scream has made it out of my mouth. Instead, I am reported to have a look of pure terror on my face while my mouth soundlessly hangs open.

When I was in college my roommate decided to play a trick on me. I was showering in the communal bathroom on a Friday night around 11:00 p.m. No one else was in the bathroom, and I had my towel slung over the side of the shower. All of a sudden I saw my towel yanked over the curtain and onto the other side. Immediately I thought it was a prank from a drunken floor mate, and I had absolutely no idea what to do because I had left the rest of my clothes and my robe in my room. I was so terrified that my mouth opened but I couldn't speak. After a second or two I heard my roommate's voice say, "Aww, Jessie! You didn't even react!"

I laughed as if I wasn't fazed and thought, *If you only knew.*

It wasn't until recently that I started being able to scream when startled. I consider it quite an accomplishment. The most notable example was the summer I moved into an apartment inhabited by both my dear friend and a number of fearless roaches. I was definitely not a fan, but I had decided to not let that ruin my opportunity to live in a cute apartment downtown within walking distance of some of my favorite spots and share daily life with one of my favorite people. However, a few nights after I moved in, I saw a rather large roach come scuttling out of Kacie's doorway. As she was talking, I told her to hold on and went to go grab a shoe to deliver the death penalty. (Yes, if you're a roach trespassing around these parts, you've been pre-tried and found guilty.) The problem was that before I could deliver the smack down, it ran under the rug beneath Kacie's bed. Prior to this moment, it was a nuisance, kind of gross, slightly frustrating.

At this moment, the situation escalated. Now there was a good-sized roach that was MIA somewhere underneath Kacie's bed. We started plotting about how to draw it out because there was no way she was going to go to sleep now. As we tried to come up with solutions, Kacie went on about, "My bed! My warm, cozy bed! I can't believe it! That nasty thing probably crawled up in my bed by now!" We contemplated moving the bed, but then we'd have to move all the boxes stored neatly underneath. And roaches can stay put where they are for hours upon hours, so it might not venture out anytime soon. Finally we decided to try the vacuum cleaner. Kacie needed to vacuum her room anyway, so she started vacuuming around the bed while I stood next to it, poised and waiting with a shoe. However, the element of surprise is quite an advantage on the side of a slick and speedy roach, and even though we were in fact waiting in the hopes of smacking said roach on its appearance, the moment it emerged from under the rug we let out a giant, unison "Ahhhhhhh!" three times in succession, as I proceeded to *smack, smack, smack!* Finally the roach was still.

Unfortunately, the problem was not completely solved. Now we had a giant dead roach on the carpet. I told Kacie that since I killed it, it was her job to pick it up and put it in the trash. She attempted to pick it up, using her Chaco sandals like chopsticks, but every time she tried, she dropped it and shuddered. "I hear it crunching!" she exclaimed. After the third attempt, I gave her the trash bag, and I picked it up with her Chacos.

A few weeks later we found another one in our bathroom. It was too high up on the ceiling for us to reach, so Kacie went next door to go get Kyle (our newly contracted roach killer, who took care of the dirty work for us in exchange for cookies and specialty sodas from a local grocery store). I stood guard at the bathroom door to make sure it didn't escape. Right before Kacie stepped out of the house, I looked up and saw the roach flying toward me and screamed yet again as I slammed the bathroom door. I told Kacie we had a flying roach on our hands, and she ran even faster to go get the "expert." I left the bathroom door closed, eyeing the three-inch crack at the bottom, with a shoe in my hand. If the roach was coming out, it would have to come out crawling, and then I'd get it. A minute or two later Kacie arrived with Kyle, and he tracked it down in the bathroom, taking care of it with one fell swoop of a boot. (In our defense, he was even impressed with its size.)

Though spiders and critters rarely made me scream, I was plenty good at asking for extermination help when I was growing up. Dad knew the intonation of my voice that told him, "Hurry up, there's a spider or other gross critter in here!" In actuality, it was a two-toned version of "DAA-aaaaaad!" After issuing a call like that, I would hear the thump of Dad's footsteps heading my way, and he'd call out, "Do you have a Kleenex for me to use?" When he arrived, he'd proceed to take the Kleenex and say, "Sorry, little guy, I don't want to kill you, but Jessie says you have to go." One time an icky spider encroached on my shower and I had to jump out to go get Dad. I told him, "I just met a spider in the shower." He responded, "Oh really? What was his name?"

When Dad wasn't home, Mom usually rescued me from the critters. Sometimes, though, if she tried to smush them and they jumped away, she'd give a short "Ah! Ah!" until they were safely contained in the Kleenex.

Nowadays I have to smack my own roaches and smush my own spiders. Even before Dad died, he was a thousand miles away, and at the end of the summer Kyle moved out of the house next door. I guess it's part of growing up, but some days it's one more reminder I have to face this world alone. Granted, it's always a happy day when Kacie and I are able to battle the roaches together, but at the end of the day, she's my roommate. She's not responsible for feeding me when I'm weak and tired or doing my laundry when I'm so exhausted all I can do is lay on the couch in my pajamas. It's not up to her to pay my bills or grocery shop for me or even to help me process life. She's a true kindred spirit, so some days she does make dinner for us or fold my laundry, and most days she sits and listens to me process what's on my mind. But it's not her job (or anyone else's) to take care of me, so I have to protect others from feeling that responsibility.

This is why I keep my screams locked inside. I want to be free but I don't want to be treated differently. As I let pain and anger out, I don't want anyone else to take them on, and for Pete's sake I do not want to be pitied. I'm changing, though. My progress is slow, but I'm starting to acknowledge there are people in my life I can scream around. I haven't actually tried it yet, but someday I will. One day I'll have the courage to release a roar that starts in my toes and then let it grow to a shriek of eardrum-shattering proportions. I'll yell until my voice is hoarse and my lungs gasp for air. Then I will walk out of the shadows and into the sunlight, close my eyes, and laugh.

Like Fabric, Like Vapor

"Take off that shirt! Take it off right now and give it back!" I shouted in my mind. On the outside I said nothing, but the intensity of my gaze was a dead giveaway to anyone who knew me well enough to notice it. The anger was a rock in my chest, heavy and immovable.

This woman was wearing my dad's shirt.

My dead father's souvenir T-shirt with a desert sunset and screen printed "Sedona, AZ" had been appropriated by a stranger. An amicable student at the discipleship program I used to work for and the exact person making small talk with me at that very minute, she was entirely clueless about the origin of the shirt she wore. This wasn't a case of *Gilmore Girls* confusion, where Lorelai Gilmore obliviously pulls Luke's ex-girlfriend's sweatshirt out of the rummage sale bin and wears it into his diner. No, this was entirely different. Luke put that sweatshirt in the rummage sale donations. He didn't want it, and he didn't want to see it anymore. When we sorted through my dad's clothing after he died, I chose to save this particular T-shirt as a memory of our annual spring break trips spent hiking mesas, climbing the rocks next to Oak Creek, and dining on fine Mexican fare at El Rincon. I had not given this shirt away. Prior to this morning, I believed the shirt was safely stored with my other things in the attic. But here it was resting on someone else's frame.

How on earth could this have happened? Who would have dug my dad's shirt out of my things and moved it to the donated clothing section of the attic for a student to claim? And if that shirt was gone, how many other precious things had migrated from my blatantly labeled storage tubs carefully clustered far away from the students' suitcases, the Christmas decorations, and the clothing closet?

When Dad died, I didn't have enough space in my tiny staff apartment for Grandma's china, my childhood toys, Dad's things, and everything else I wasn't ready to let go of, so the directors let me store my things in the attic of the staff/student housing where I lived. When I moved off campus into my small apartment, I hardly had room for a café table and sectional in the living/dining room and some mismatched plates and mugs in the kitchen, let alone my heirloom furnishings and mementos. It was a relief to have the opportunity to leave everything there until I moved into a larger space.

Well, it had been a relief to store my things there.

It wasn't until I climbed the steps into the suffocating heat and stared into the dim light coming from a single light bulb that I put together what must have happened. There was a strange T-shirt on top of one of my boxes. It was a rectangle cardboard box filled with paper files and no lid. Next to it was a pile of random clothes. They didn't belong there—that was it. I had tucked the T-shirt into the top of the box, hoping it would keep roaches and spiders out. Someone accidentally placed the clothing next to my things, and when a student was looking through it for more T-shirts, she thought the one on top of my box was part of the pile.

It was an honest mistake.

So why did the heavy weight swing against the sides of my chest as I drove away? Why did my cheeks burn and my eyes fight back tears when the staff member on duty returned my call and I explained what happened? Why didn't her assurances that my dad's shirt would be washed and returned restore my peace?

That shirt was not there for her—or anyone else—to take. It was mine. It was mine just like Grandma Teach's china and Danish collector plates, Mom's sewing machine, Dad's skis, Grandpa Don's books, and Grandma Shirley's jewelry. These things belonged to me just like those people belonged to me. They were my family. I never even got to meet Grandma Teach. She died before she had a chance to see my dad graduate from college and law school and get married, just like my own mom. My mother missed my senior prom, high school graduation, and college graduation, and she will miss every other landmark event in the years to come. It was too soon to say good-bye to her mother just a year later and to Dad's dad months after that. And nobody was prepared to write Dad's obituary just four years from Grandpa's memorial.

When I look at the people around me, I wonder when each lovely season of companionship will end. What will it cost me? How much will it hurt? Nobody gets to stay forever. And so with every precious soul friend I gain, I bear the dread of the day our paths will diverge and the unavoidable moment when we can no longer see each other's faces, followed by the point where our voices can no longer penetrate the foliage and one more dear one is lost.

To open one's heart is to become so very exposed. To need people is so terrifyingly vulnerable. I sometimes wonder if I cut ties with every person who has ever made my heart sing with laughter and went off to live by myself, hidden away in the mountains, would I be immune to the taking and the losing? Could I build a fortress strong and secretive enough that the robber couldn't find me, and even if he did, my gate would hold against a thousand years of battering rams?

Some people say life isn't about waiting out the rough patches but rather learning to laugh and dance in the midst of them. This isn't so hard when it rains in the middle of a drought or an afternoon shower glides through, but what about when the refreshing rains become raging rivers? Who can sing when fields are flattened and gardens littered with petals? Find me someone who dances when sliding mud swallows home and earthly possessions.

I want to be Job, the man who bows his head in reverence in response to the news that his children have suddenly died. It would be so much easier if I could declare it is the Lord's prerogative to give and to take and bless Him for it, but the truth is I'm just so tired of the taking. I don't think I can bear much more of it. Even now I feel as though just a shadow of myself is left. If I were a vapor, a modest puff of air could disperse me in a moment. Spontaneous dance no longer compels my limbs to move. Reverberations of the soul rarely glide between my lips. My brilliant brain lies mostly beneath a cloud of fog. No amount of sleep refreshes me. There are moments when laughter bubbles up from the deep places and I can feel, but mostly my insides are just numb. It's hard to feel much of anything over the sensation of losing—sometimes clenching sometimes searing but always constant and never ending.

Section Four

Striding

Just call me a mess. It's okay. Go ahead and say it. I can't seem to get it together. Every time I get close or start to hit my stride, that one loose string gets pulled or my shoe hits the wobbly cobblestone and *boom*—the whole sweater unravels. I go down, knees splayed, arms flailing, falling.

Again.

It's not as far to fall as when I lost my balance and tumbled off that cliff, not quite as shocking as when my pale skin hit the top layer of water and it punched the breath out of me. No, it's not nearly as dangerous as when the icy water rushed over my head and I froze.

It's not that serious, no potentially fatal wounds.

So why can't I just get up and keep walking? How do I fall beneath the concrete on every trip, searching for a manhole to climb back out of? Will I never find my stride and keep it again?

When I was growing up my family used to take a ski trip every year. Once I outgrew the ski center daycare program, I went to ski school during the day. There I learned from an instructor with several other kids around the same skill level. We'd take turns falling on the way down the hill as we skied in a line, attempting to follow the instructions shouted over our leader's shoulder to "Pizza pie, French fry!" (or keep skis parallel and straight across the hill, turn them into a wedge to make the turn, and then go straight across the hill again). I took a lot of falls in those days and had my skis pop off more than a few times, but I kept getting up, and over the years the falls became less and less. The last time I went on a ski trip with my dad in Montana, I may have fallen once in the fresh powder snow because that stuff is so thick you have to ski through it differently. As I skied with Dad, I no longer alternated between pizza pie and French fry moves. Instead I pointed my shoulders downhill, and my feet slid left and right, my heels running a windshield-wiper pattern underneath me as I made rapid turns in a rhythm that went *swish, swish, swish*. I held my poles out in front of me for balance, planting them at the point of each turn as my legs reached the deepest part of my squat, forcing the skis around the turn before standing up and repeating the drill: right, left, right, left. Occasionally I got tired and stopped to take in the view and catch my breath, my thighs burning from the exertion, but nothing else broke my stride. This was my adrenaline rush. Forget rollercoasters; I loved flying down the mountain—free, yet safe because I was in control.

Control is a tricky thing, though. The more urgently I grapple for it, the faster it seems to slide through my fingers. I never seem to be able to control the things I really want, and settling for manipulating what is within reach never really quenches fear or satisfies anxiety. A questionnaire at my doctor's office a year ago asked what I am most afraid of. My answer was not death, not public speaking, not even losing more people I love (although that's probably number two)—I am most afraid of losing control to the point that as a mature twenty-something woman, I am completely unable to take care of myself.

This happens when you've experienced fatigue so intense that you lay on the couch for hours, telling yourself you have to get up and eat food, but your body is so heavy that it's easier to just lay there and not eat. It's the fear that grips tighter every time someone says you look like you have energy and praises you for how skinny you are, while your foggy brain struggles to focus on the things they're saying and you know you dropped past your healthy weight several pounds ago. And then there's the looks, the judgments, the questions: "How can you be so sick if you look fine?" "Why can't you pull it together?" "Are you ever going to go back to work?" "What would your parents think about this?" And so the anxiety grows every time you have to be around people who don't regularly see you, the ones who can't read the fatigue in your unfocused eyes and the depression in your shorter-than-normal responses. For if you truly lose it, they won't be there for you because they think you're fine. And yet it's not really true. People don't say these things. Aside from one or two, their looks don't mean they disapprove of you. They don't seek information from you like crows from a corpse. These are merely the things you feel.

These are the things *we* feel, those of us with another voice in our ears, a different set of eyes in which we see disapproval, an iron will from which we receive judgment. They are our own, every one of them. We have honed their skills to form a shield around us. As long as we disapprove of our progress, we dull the sting of other's disapproval. If we reject ourselves first, we beat them to it. If we play the discouraged one who recognizes where she or he ought to be and is sufficiently frustrated with it, we will receive encouragement and support rather than a shattering rebuke.

This is why I must drive myself on through the healing process. There is no time to waste. There is music to be played, people who need help, books to write, Bible studies to lead, jobs to be worked, financial stability to be had, and so much more. It's all waiting for me. It's time to go. I've rested long enough.

But then there's this voice in my head that says I've never

really rested. Though I slowed from a sprint to a jog to a walk, I haven't stopped, except for the moments when I fell splat on the pavement. Even then, the second my momentum stopped siding with gravity, I wanted to reverse its direction.

True rest requires a safe place. In that rest there is stillness, acceptance, contentment combined with the knowledge that this moment is fleeting, and the deep desire to savor it before it fades. So no, I have not rested. I have gritted my teeth, alternating between throwing myself into activities that promote healing and losing myself in entertainment, all the while hoping that I would wake up one day and find my body ready to run again.

Split for Survival

I reach for life, for abounding joy that I've held once before. For a moment I touch it, gently cradle it in my palm, and then launch it into the air above my head. As it falls, it swirls around me, covering me like a handful of glitter.

The thing with glitter, though, is that it stays. Even glitter without glue attaches itself to human skin with the most persistent of bonds; if I brush it off my arm, it becomes stuck to my hand. Why can't joy be more like glitter? It slips away so quickly at the most inopportune moments, here for a few brilliant hours or days and then nothing more than a breath of memory.

What is it that displaces joy with sandy grit? What ties me to the banks of the river where I become maker of mud pies instead of swimming in the clear water?

Self, what is it? What could have started this cycle of fatigue and depression?

Do you really want to know?

Yes, of course. I wouldn't ask if I didn't.

I've been waiting for you to ask, so I will tell you, but I don't think you'll like the answer.

I'll like it just fine. Nothing you say can shake me.

I'm still trapped in the storms of the past.

Surely not, I saw sunshine outside my window only this morning. There are no storms here. I've survived them and built a new life again.

Yes, you have tried to build a new life. You may not sit under the cloudy deluge. Sandbags may not surround your house, but I didn't say you were still trapped in the storms of the past. I said I was.

This can't be; you and I are the same. Where I go, you go, too.

You are right that it's meant to be that way. Once we walked together, but there came a time when that is not how you wanted it. You walked on ahead and told me to stay behind. You didn't like the things I saw and heard and didn't want to be reminded of them, so you left me behind and went on to find a place where the sun always shone, the clouds never cried, and "flood" was a five letter word.

When? When did I do this?

It began when Mom moved out of our house, not because of a strained relationship with Dad but because of faulty bone marrow. It really started a year before that, though. It started when Mom was sick all summer and the diagnosis finally landed on myelodysplastic syndrome. It began when I was reprimanded for telling someone over the phone that my mom was having a hysterectomy. This was a private matter, they said. I wasn't supposed to tell. I hadn't volunteered that information, but I was fifteen and I didn't know what to say when the woman I babysat for asked what kind of surgery my mom was having.

I barely remember that. It was so long ago. So much time has passed since then. It doesn't matter anymore.

You barely remember it because I remember it for you. It doesn't have to matter to you because it matters to me. Don't you see?

No, I don't. You remember it because it matters to you. If it doesn't matter to me, why must I remember it?

Let me continue. This story is far from over. A year later Mom's numbers of incorrect blood cells or "blasts" skyrocketed, and she moved to the chemo floor in the hospital downtown. In order to heal her, they had to kill her immune system. While her insides slowly died, I learned to survive on my own. Every morning I packed my own lunch and melted cheese on a bagel or buttered toast to take with me, leaving the house before Dad woke up for the day. The next six and a half hours I wrote essays and papers, took lecture notes, completed quizzes, and answered questions. After school I changed into tennis gear in the locker room and drove to practice. I arrived home around the same time as Dad, so we cooked tilapia, shrimp, or meatballs and some vegetables for dinner. We usually returned home from the hospital around 8:00 or 9:00 p.m. At that point I started my homework. I was taking two college-level courses, and my other private school classes were no joke, so homework took at least three hours every night. I often put in a few loads of laundry while I worked at the kitchen table so that Dad and I had clean clothes. Sometimes I took a break to iron his shirts. Around midnight or 1:00 a.m. I went to bed and caught a few precious hours of sleep before the alarm went off around 6:30 a.m., and I did it all over again.

That certainly was a lot of work to manage, but

many people do that, especially college students. It was only for a season; you got through it.

Might I mention I was sixteen? That we celebrated my seventeenth birthday around Mom's bed in the hospital? Do I have to state the obvious that although I had my driver's license, I was still very much in need of care from Mom and Dad, but instead I was taking care of myself and them?

Okay, you were young. You shouldn't have had to do those things, but Dad retired a few months after the chemo started, and he began doing your laundry and taking care of Mom.

Yes, but he didn't know how to take care of me. One day I was so sick. I had really bad period cramps and was in terrible pain at school. Lunchtime found me so nauseated that I couldn't eat a thing, and I hurt so bad that two friends had to sling my arms over their shoulders and half carry me to the nurse's office. After a half hour nap and some ibuprofen, I still felt terrible. I needed to go home, but the nurse and I were debating whether I was well enough to drive myself. Mom was in the hospital, and Dad was at work. My best friend, Alli, worked out a plan with her mom where she would drive me home in my car, and her mom would pick her up from my house and drive her back to school. I ended up rallying enough to make it the three miles home then sink onto the couch with an afghan and a movie. Alli's mom dropped off a care package with some snacks and even cut up an orange for me. It meant a lot, but I didn't want Alli's mom that day. I wanted my mom.

I wanted Mom the day I came inside halfway through mowing the lawn because I had cramps again, and Dad had the audacity to ask me if it hurt worse standing up and mowing than laying on the couch.

I needed Mom the day I tried to explain to Dad how overwhelmed I felt as we drove home from visiting Grandpa. Taking care of both Lindsey's and my household-cleaning lists each week in addition to school, sports, and homework was too much. He asked how many hours a week it took to complete the lists. I told him two. And then he asked, "Is it really too much to ask you to help out around the house for two hours a week?" Checkmate. I had no choice but to say, "No, Dad, it's not," my iron gaze piercing the windshield. The victory had been within my grasp, but I had to expose my queen to claim it and that was something I simply could not do.

Okay, that stunk. Dad wasn't the most sensitive person, and he didn't "get" you, but Mom wasn't in the hospital that long, only a few months at a time and then she came home for several long stretches.

Mom came home, yes, but she came home sick, and none of the nurses from the hospital accompanied her. She slept on the couch because she had a hard time with the stairs, and Dad slept on Lindsey's twin mattress on the floor of the living room so that he could help her get up off the couch and walk to the bathroom in the middle of the night. On evenings when Dad wanted to take a short break and go out for dinner with a friend, I had to stay at home with Mom. When she started to panic about having to go to the bathroom, I had to calmly but firmly grasp her forearms and lift her off the couch as she sucked in painful breaths from the two stress fractures in her back, which we were unaware of. I had to support her as she walked to the bathroom and help her slowly lower to sit on the toilet.

Dad took the brunt of taking care of Mom. How could you complain about having to help her out a few times while Dad went to dinner? She changed your diapers and cleaned up your puke for years. You're going to complain about having to help her walk to the bathroom and sit down on the toilet a few times?

It's so much more than that, if you'll just try to remember. I wasn't merely the objective helper. I was witness. On those nights when her system rebelled against self-control as a result of the graft-versus-host disease and she couldn't make it all the way to the bathroom, it was me who saw. Yes, seventeen and eighteen-year-old me were the witnesses.

Need I continue? Need I talk about what went on in the hospital rooms? The ordinary days (if any can be called that) don't stick in my memory. The ones that remain are the awful days. I remember the time I found a bug in the car on the way to the hospital and thought it went out of the car, but it actually found a home in my purse. When we got into Mom's room with our masks in tact and hands washed clean, it emerged and jumped around the room until Dad killed it. Mom shrieked, terrified of the germs, and I was scolded.

There was the day when we arrived, and Mom sat on the bed crying. Despite the silk pillowcase and every effort to slow the chemo's effects on her hair, the thick brown strands were falling out faster than the nurses could keep up with. The night before, a nurse had to cut the dead hair off the wheels of her IV stand because she was too weak to roll it around the room. She was crying because that evening, one day later, the wheels were already hard to move again.

In the brief interval between hospital stays there was the day Mom and Dad went to the wig shop. She was happy with her choice, but she cried as she told me how the woman had to cut the last matted chunk of hair off the back of her head so the wig would fit. She lost the last bit of her own hair in order to comfortably wear the fake hair.

Do you remember? Please, tell me I'm not the only one who holds these memories.

I don't want to remember. I thought remembering was your job so that living could be mine.

I can't hold them alone anymore. I can't do it. I'm not that strong, and that was never meant to be my job. You will never find true life as long as you force me to carry the memories.

You must know there were good memories, too, or at least ones that should have been precious, like the day Mom realized she had a birthmark on the back of her head that extended a little way down her neck in the same place as mine. She never noticed it before because her hair had always covered it. She was wearing a soft fleece cap instead of a wig the day she told me this. As she pulled the cap off all I saw was her bare scalp. She pointed to the birthmark, but I couldn't see it through the absence of her hair.

I was standing in that same room the day she was having a graft-versus-host flare-up and the stem cells were attacking her gut especially hard. She had to go to the bathroom and needed the nurses' help to get from the bed to the potty chair. Making it all the way to the bathroom on the other side of the room was out of the question. She pushed the button, but they weren't coming. Panic set in because she knew what was going to happen if they didn't arrive soon. Dad hollered down the hallway for someone to come help his wife. Finally they arrived, but as they got her up to walk, her body betrayed her and left a trail of blood from the bed to the chair. Once she was settled the nurses cleaned it up. They didn't react; they remained calm. This wasn't a big deal to them, but those spots of blood are burned into my mind. I can still see those traitorous spots of blood on the floor.

Do you believe me? Do you believe me now?

Stop—that's enough. I believe you. I know it happened. I don't want to hear any more.

No, you don't really believe me. You don't believe this is evidence enough for the weeks at a time you've struggled to get out of bed because your body is so weighed down by these toxic memories, and your heart can't seem to rid itself of the road rash left behind by grief and trauma.

I won't stop until you really get it. Put your hands down. Even if you blew your eardrums to pieces with dynamite, it wouldn't work. The sound of my voice will keep ringing between your temples until you hear everything I have to say.

You must remember the last time she was in the hospital, when they discovered a tiny piece of fungus that had invaded her lungs. It grew and grew. They had to put a tube down her throat so a machine could breath for her. This meant she couldn't talk. It was my senior year of high school. I was less than two months away from graduation, and when I, her youngest daughter, her namesake, wore my new bright blue Drake University sweatshirt into her hospital room and told her I had decided to go to Drake, all she could do was give me a thumbs up.

I don't think she was conscious by the time a friend asked me to spring formal. Her struggle to breathe had become so traumatic and painful that the doctors decided to put her in a medically induced coma. Nurses took turns monitoring her twenty-four hours a day, suctioning blood out of her lungs when her breathing started to gurgle. Once a day they brought her out of the coma to monitor her. Dad wanted to be there when they did it, so that she could see familiar faces and hear our voices talking to her while she was awake for those few brief minutes. I just wanted to leave. The peace and calm that was over her body when she was in the coma fled when they brought her to consciousness, and the excruciating pain and fear that swooped in were too much to witness.

I heard Dad cry for the first time in my life the morning Mom died. No one else was there in the wee hours of March 27, 2008, when we returned home from the hospital with Mom's things and Dad called her parents to tell them the news. He only got out the words "Janet's gone" before he broke down in the biggest sobs I have ever heard. He was standing in the dining room about twenty feet from where I laid on the couch in the family room, watching TV because I *couldn't sleep. I didn't go to him, though. I think I was already numb or maybe just trying to respect his space. I don't know what Grandma and Grandpa said to him. I just know it was dark and she was gone, but he was there and I was there, and I'm not sure either of us knew what to do about that.*

Dad and I never talked about the events of that night. I never said a word to him about anything that happened at the hospital. I cried and yelled about some of it to Alli, but I never said a word to Dad.

I told Lindsey what transpired that morning when we arrived at the hospital too late, but I never described to her what took place at the hospital while she was at college. I never gave her the visual backdrop to her conversations on the phone with Mom.

Why didn't you talk to them?

Lindsey had to deal with the shock of how much Mom changed between her visits home. Dad saw even more than I did. They had burdens enough. The thing is, I can't do it anymore, though. I can't protect them, and I can't protect you.

Why?

You want to be alive, to live a life of joy, don't you?

Yes, I want that so much it hurts sometimes.

I can't protect you anymore, because you cannot be alive to joy if you refuse to embrace pain. You will remain fearful of loss until you wrap your arms around this ball of fire and allow it to burn through you—through me—and make us one again.

And Then There Was One

It was a day set apart to celebrate two becoming one: two lives, hearts, purposes, and dreams joining together. I was there because I always said I would be there, ever since the days when Lauren and I spent dreamy summer afternoons reading in her hammock and evenings becoming prunes in her hot tub. We wrote about it in notes exchanged between seventh-grade English and tenth-grade AP US History. We crafted stories about who each one would be and the trail of events that would lead up to us vowing to love at all costs this man who would stand before us at the altar. We knew we'd be there to witness these ceremonies for each other, standing up front in a pretty dress of our choosing and discreetly or not so discreetly swiping away happy tears.

It took me twenty-three hours of driving and stopping, over the course of two and a half days, to make it to Camp Lakamaga in Minnesota. I pulled into a dirt parking space, my little red car topped with two red-orange kayaks that I prayed would stay tied down all the way back to their new home in Tennessee. Stepping out of the car at ten minutes to five o'clock, I fluffed my lacy coral dress so it wouldn't stick to my legs as I headed in the direction everyone else was going.

The ceremony began with Drew escorting his grandmother down the aisle. I identified him from photos I'd seen of them together. I didn't recognize the first two bridesmaids, but next were JoJo and Elizabeth, classmates of ours from high school and years of Sunday school, also roommates of Lauren's for the last year. Elsie was next. I had met her once before when I visited Lauren's dorm at college. Finally came Amy, the maid of honor, another friend of ours from high school. Their dresses were all different yet flattering to each woman in their varying shades and styles of gray.

The moment we had been waiting for came when we spotted Lauren and her father strolling across the field. She was absolutely beautiful, no longer the baby-faced junior higher with braces and "poofy" hair. No, this Lauren had bangs and loose curls draped over her shoulders. Her lace-bodice dress with a flowing satin skirt highlighted her slender feminine frame, and her smile could not have been any bigger. Somewhere in the middle of Drew's vows she couldn't contain the happy tears anymore, and they streamed down her face as she stared into his eyes, the microphone picking up her short sobs.

I wanted to be there. I wouldn't have come all that way if I didn't. Yet, when the last chord of the recessional faded into the muggy summer air, I found my feet longing to turn in the direction of my car instead of the reception. I had no desire to make small talk with so many people who were a part of my life before.

I had made a new life for myself in Tennessee, one I quite enjoyed. Several days a week I spent the morning or afternoon writing at my favorite coffee shop, where they prepared my "usual" (café au lait with almond milk) and never charged extra for the milk substitution. Monday nights I slipped on my vintage dancing sneakers, triple stepping my way through Lindy Hop and kicking up a storm with the Charleston. On summer evenings I strolled down Oak Street to the courthouse and back with my kindred spirit roommate, and random Saturdays I set out hiking with friends in the foothills of the Appalachian Mountains.

I belonged in Tennessee, not Minnesota like everyone else, but the naked truth of the matter was that my decision to call Tennessee home was not the reason I felt out of step with this hub of people I grew up with. I didn't fit in their crowd because I was only one. The reception room was filled with Lauren's family and her parents' friends and their children who are her friends. They came in twos, threes, fours, even sixes, but I came alone. Everyone was so excited to see me—friends and parents alike—shouting my name and hugging me. They asked about life in Tennessee and how my sister and I were doing. Amy said it was so good to see me and she wanted to catch up. We discovered Laura lives three miles from my sister in Dallas. She said I had to let her know next time I was in town so that we could get together. As I returned their smiles and hugs, not one understood what I couldn't say: that as long as I was alive in their presence, I would be one of three who ought to be there. My name was written on the guest list underneath my parents' names, and when theirs were crossed out, the pen ran through mine, too.

You see, in the days that Lauren and I dreamed of picking out wedding dresses and being each other's bridesmaids, I lived with my parents in a house on a golf course, five minutes away from Lauren's home. We attended the same church my mother had gone to since her parents moved to that suburb in the seventies, and I went to the school where Lauren and I started kindergarten and continued the next thirteen years of our education. As we became best friends and my older sister went off to college, our parents became friends, too. The six of us even took a ski trip together out to Montana. When Lauren and I looked to the future, we saw ourselves going to college and coming home on breaks to see our families and each other. We assumed we would meet men in college who loved the Lord and us and get married the summer after we graduated. We would live close by and write and drink tea and watch *Anne of Green Gables* and be wives, mothers, and kindred spirits for the years to come.

But that didn't happen. Our eleventh grade year I chose to take advanced classes and Lauren didn't, which meant we didn't have any classes together. The fall of that year my mom began her treatment for MDS. When Lauren called and invited me to hang out on weeknights that I didn't have basketball or tennis, I usually declined, because after making dinner with my dad I had to go visit Mom at the hospital and then do my homework. Three months after we graduated high school, I went off to college in Des Moines, Iowa, and Lauren went to a school in the Twin Cities. I widened the distance when I moved to Tennessee after college and spent most of my short Minnesota visits with my family.

This was so much more than just a friendship that faded with time and distance, though. The plan we dreamed up for our lives was destroyed for me. It would never be. When I looked at Lauren, I saw her walking out our dreams without me. Her parents still went to the same church and resided in the same house. She still lives in the Twin Cities and spent the last year sharing a house with friends from our high school days. She met her hubby in college, and though she didn't marry him the summer after graduation, as of today she is Lauren Elrick. She is passionate and full of life and love, a freelance writer and a poet.

I didn't expect her to ask me to be a bridesmaid. In reality I wasn't sure I'd even be invited to the wedding. I couldn't help but feel that it was all wrong, though, as I sat in the audience and watched Lauren pledge her life to loving Drew, a man I had heard about but never met. It should have been me standing next to her in a gray dress. My parents should have sat in the crowd beaming at both of us. It wasn't right that I met Drew on the dance floor of their wedding reception, or that I won bragging rights as the person who traveled the farthest to get there. Why did I have to drive alone and stand just outside the circle of dancing couples under the navy sky? Why did they have to die so soon, long before they wanted to go, even longer before I was prepared to say goodbye?

Will their absence always stand like a glassy pane between those who would love me and my fiery independent heart? Will I ever truly be more than one again?

Epilogue

Tomorrow

This morning as I slowly woke up, eyes still closed and body tucked between microfiber sheets, the first thing I heard was a chorus of birds trilling outside my window. Our air conditioning hasn't been working this week, so I've slept with the windows open all night for the first time in a long, long time. For a few minutes, as I lay there listening to the birds, I was waking up in a loft bedroom, with the sliding glass door halfway open, bird songs around me punctuated by the blinds smacking against the door frame in the light morning breeze and a few lone jet skis zinging across the early morning water.

I've been dreaming about the cabin lately, that lovely little abode full of rest, peace, and wonderful memories. The dreams have been strange, though. In them, I go back for a visit with several friends. I let us in with my keys, and we enjoy our visit immensely, until someone shows up and I realize we have to get out before we're caught, because the truck parked outside may belong to the new owners or one of their friends and we must not be discovered inside.

I suppose I shouldn't be surprised at the dreams, because they rather closely follow reality. Lindsey and I sold the cabin last summer. We loved it but simply could not keep it. I live a thousand miles away from Comstock, Wisconsin, and Lindsey is almost equidistant in Dallas, Texas. Once Dad died we weren't able to get up there very often, and it really wasn't worth spending several thousand dollars annually to maintain a vacation home we visited a week or two each year. We told ourselves we could go on many wonderful adventures for that price and acknowledged that being at the cabin wasn't the same without Mom and Dad. We also considered the difficulty of finding a friend to go meet the plumber when something went wrong and the hassles of owning a house built by the men who lived around the lake sixty years ago. Yes, it was definitely the most practical and financially responsible decision.

I still miss it, though.

The cabin was a haven, a place of refuge from the stress of jobs and school across the state line. Dad originally bought it because he wanted us to experience what he had growing up. Every summer his whole extended family went up to Woman Lake in northern Minnesota and rented cabins for two weeks. They had cookouts, water-skied, and fished, and the cousins exchanged comic books. He also craved a place to get away from the stress of his job as a corporate lawyer. The cabin wasn't all play; we did work, too, but it wasn't mentally demanding work. That's the place where Lindsey and I learned how to take down wallpaper and paint rooms. We also painted the outside of the cabin, the garage doors, and even the boathouse. Every spring we took the storm windows off the three-season porch; in summers we mowed the lawn and scraped moss off outdoor carpeting. In the fall we raked huge piles of leaves to jump in before carting them into the woods, and one winter we even helped Dad shovel snow off the roof.

So many of my good memories with Dad happened at the cabin. It was a place where he truly got to be a dad, laughing as he drove the boat in donuts around the lake, trying to sling me off the tube; meeting in hand-to-hand combat over an intense game of cribbage; and canoeing around the island at dusk.

For the most part, cabin memories of Mom are good, too. The summer of her illness she was not well enough to go swimming, but it was the most "normal" season we had with her after the stem-cell transplant. She was home all summer, so she didn't miss any cabin trips. Dad set up air purifiers in their bedroom so she could eat meals in there and spend the rest of the time with us, accompanied by her bright blue-green mask.

When Dad died and left me and Lindsey the cabin, we decided it would be too sad to visit by ourselves. We needed to reinvent it with new memories of time spent there with friends and family. For the most part we succeeded. Aunt Teddi and Uncle Eric faithfully came whenever we invited, Teddi planning meals and Eric assisting in handyman chores. We invited other friends, as well, and thoroughly enjoyed our time there, but it was different. One of the things about spending time at the cabin that was so relaxing to me was sitting on the porch, reading a book for hours in the afternoon, or laying on the pier in the sun as the sounds of the lake floated around me. Technically nothing kept me from doing these things, but when we had company we didn't often see, it felt selfish to sneak away and read for hours by myself. I also couldn't help but feel like I was waiting every afternoon for Mom to yell down from the screened porch, "Girls, can you come shuck corn?" or another dinner preparation request, and when I smelled burgers on the grill, I always expected to see Dad close by, taking in the sunset over the water while flipping the juiciest burgers I ever ate.

For everything there is a season. I knew last summer the

season of the cabin was ending. It was more than just the cabin, though. In many ways it marked the official ending of my childhood. That was the last place where I got to be a kid. I didn't have to do all the cooking and cleaning or wash all the dishes. Someone else was there to help take care of the sump pump or leaky faucet issue. All that ended when I signed my name on the selling agreement.

Now I look around me and see the life I have made for myself in the last nine years. It doesn't look much like I imagined, with plenty of things I wish were different. Yet, I also see beauty, simplicity, and depth that I could not have fathomed.

Learning to live in this reality calls for messy courage. It issues the challenge to expand beyond grief and sadness, asking of me, "Can you hold with open hands these delightful and difficult things you've been given? Will you treasure what is before you today and let go of what was only meant for yesterday?"

As I look to the future, I ask myself, *Can you take the risk of loving with open hands? Can you surrender the reality you wish for and accept what exists in this present moment? Will you allow waking up to the sound of birds on a summer morning to present a tender remembrance instead of a piercing loss?*

Acknowledgments

Writing a section like this terrifies me because I know I will leave someone out or fail to convey the depth of my appreciation. That said, here is a deeply heartfelt thank you to those who have walked with me during the last ten years, through grieving and healing, struggle and breakthrough. Please know your support has been integral to the creation of this collection of essays.

Angela—Oh, the memories of hours spent writing across the table from you, sipping café au laits, and taking breaks for walks outside in the sunshine when the emotions were too bold to transfer to the page. I cannot express how grateful I am that you walked through every step of this writing and editing process alongside me. Your presence has infused me with courage and clarity at the moments when my own supply waned.

Kacie—Living with you for two years is one of the sweetest blessings I have ever received. I'll never forget the night I told you the details about my mom's sickness and death. We were kindred spirits from the beginning, but that night as you cried with me, the deeper places opened up in our friendship. Your encouragement after that to write about what happened gave me the nerve to face the terror of the empty page. Thank you for listening to me read almost every piece I wrote and for your amazing insights and critiques along the way. Here's to many more hours writing, reading, and editing together, dearest friend.

Dearest Lindsey—I love you more than I typically have the words or courage to express. You are stunningly smart, tenacious, and beautiful. I could not have weathered these storms without you. Thank you for being not only my sister, but also my partner in life, my confidant, and my encourager. Cry-laughing with you is pretty much my favorite thing to do, but I'm learning to just plain cry with you, too. The story of us is a pretty darn good one, and I'm pumped to read the next chapter.

Mom and Dad—For all the years I wanted the last word, here it is: I love you. I miss you. I am who I am today because of you. Proud to be your daughter doesn't even begin to cut it. That day when we meet again, yeah, it's going to be out of this world. (PS: I hope you like puns because I've developed quite an affinity for them.)

Hansens, Lindbergs, Bostroms—Thank you for constant love and support throughout years of struggle and change, for open invitations to show up on your doorstep for dinner, for the garage code, and even for fridge rights. I see the provision of God in my life through the covering of your daily prayers and your eager celebration of even my smallest victories.

To all the mothers and fathers who have chosen me as their daughter—Your love has nurtured, corrected, and guided me so faithfully. When I felt the Lord promise He would raise up others in the absence of my parents, I never dreamed it would be all of you. Thank you for choosing me, for calling me daughter, for opening your hearts and homes to me, and for breaking the curse of "orphan."

Heartland Family—The fact that you claim me as your own when I've been gone far longer than I worshiped with you means more than I can say. Thank you for seeing in me so much more than a messed-up, motherless daughter and not being afraid of my ugly wounds. It was in the safety of your flock that I took the first stuttering steps toward real grieving and healing.

Vineyard People—You have shown me tangible love in the most difficult and humbling times. From delivering breakfast groceries when I was too overwhelmed by grief to shop for myself to taking care of me after surgery when I could hardly walk, you have proven that I am not alone and am loved beyond my expectations.

Teen Challenge Family—I cannot express how profoundly God ministered to me during the years I lived and worked with all of you. I came to town knowing no one yet immediately felt as though I was a part of your family. Thank you for humbly sharing your own struggles and pain so that I felt at home even in my mess. I am a different person today because you called out of me strength and honor and challenged me to walk in vulnerability when I wanted to stuff my emotions and hide.

Dr. McClanahan—I came to you fed up with fatigue, out of treatment options, and labeled with a dismal "chronic fatigue syndrome" diagnosis. Your hopeful response to fifteen pages about my chronic issues and removal of that diagnosis were game changers. I would not be traveling, hiking, and dreaming about the future again if our paths had not crossed. I'll even venture to say I wouldn't be writing this section of acknowledgments, considering the fact that I started writing again in response to the challenge you leveled to express the emotions I had so expertly concealed. Thank you.

To my counselors—Thank you for never being afraid of my trauma and grief, for providing a safe space for me to share the things I held in for so many years, and for always affirming me. You have played some of the most integral roles in my healing journey and given me the tools to extend grace to others and myself.

Thank you, Micki Ann, David, Adam, Megan, and Miss V for reading and editing pieces of this work. Your input and encouragement have been invaluable in the editing and completion process.

About the Author

J. J. Hansen is a storyteller with the spirit of a pioneer, the brain of her lawyer father, and the social graces of her mother. Born and raised in the Midwest, she studied English Writing at Drake University where she published her first essay "Strolling through a Semester in Spain" in Periphery Art and Literary Magazine. After graduation she moved to East Tennessee where she spends her time adventuring in the mountains, swing dancing in the city, and listening to stories around the dinner table. After half a decade she is still correcting locals on the pronunciation of her last name.

Printed in the United States
By Bookmasters